For Sultan

Editor
Sandrine Balihaut Martin

Design
Emmanuel Laparra

Translated from the French by
Louise Lalaurie Rogers

Copyediting
Bernard Wooding

Typesetting
Anne-Lou Bissières

Proofreading
Helen Woodhall

Color separation
Penez Éditions

Simultaneously published in French as *Broderies Marocaines*
© Éditions Flammarion, 2003
English-language edition
© Éditions Flammarion, 2003
26, rue Racine
75006 Paris

03 04 05 4 3 2 1

FC0410-03-X
ISBN: 2-0801-1173-6
Dépôt légal: 10/2003

Printed in Italy by Rotolito

ISABELLE DENAMUR

PHOTOGRAPHS BY PIERRE FERBOS

MOROCCAN
TEXTILE EMBROIDERY

Flammarion

MOROCCAN TEXTILE EMBROIDERY

CONTENTS

Page 1: *Izar* (door hanging, detail), Rabat, early-nineteenth century, monochrome silk embroidery
on embroidered cotton, length 10 ft. (300 cm), width 7 ft. (208 cm), private collection.
Pages 2–3: *Aajara* (bedcover), Tétouan, nineteenth century, satin silk damask, polychromatic silk floss embroidery,
length 5 ft. 8 in. (176 cm), width 3 ft. 9 in. (120 cm), private collection.
Facing page: *Young Woman Holding an Izar* [door hanging] *from Rabat,* Gabriel Veyre (France, 1871–1936), Jacquier-Veyre Collection, Paris.

Morocco lies at the crossroads of the African, Mediterranean, and European worlds and has been a melting pot of different civilizations. Its Islamic culture, which developed from the seventh century onward, absorbed Phoenician, Greek, Roman, Jewish, Spanish, and French elements.

These diverse influences have nourished Morocco's decorative arts. The basic geometrical forms—crosses, triangles, zigzag lines, checkerboards, starbursts, rosettes—recall African, Berber, and Coptic motifs, while the arabesques, flowers and foliage, palm fronds, traceries, and inscriptions echo Byzantine and Oriental traditions.

This synthesis of styles is particularly evident in the refined, elegant, urban art of Muslim Spain. Introduced into Spain by the Arab conquest and strengthened by the assimilation of strongly Andalusian characteristics, it combined delicate foliage, calligraphy, and floral arabesques with dazzling patterns (diamonds, polygons, foliage) and simple, powerful forms. The styles were applied to mosques and *madrasas*, palaces, city gates, townhouses, fountains, and gardens, as well as to everyday items such as furniture, jewelry, weaponry, and embroidered ceremonial costumes, clothing, and household furnishings. The styles also became one of the most distinctive features of the brilliant medieval civilization of Al-Andalus, which flourished in Córdoba, Granada, and Seville from the eighth to the fifteenth centuries under the Berber dynasties known as the Almoravids (from the Sahara) and the Almohads (from the Atlas Mountains).

Born of the desire to create a refined backdrop to everyday life, embroidery is a universal art that has chiefly been practiced by women. In Babylon, Athens, Rome, Byzantium, Baghdad, Venice, Córdoba, and Budapest, women used embroidery to add a touch of luxury to their costumes and their homes. In Morocco, embroidery has flourished (and been well documented) since the Middle Ages, particularly in the northern cities.

The materials of choice are natural silk thread—soft and downy with a fine sheen in shimmering colors obtained from natural vegetable or animal dyes—on muslin, lawn, linen, cotton, or, more rarely, silk. Despite evolving lifestyles, embroidery continues to play a prominent role in Moroccan society today. The sumptuous interiors and women's apparel that so dazzled nineteenth-century European painters are still a feature of modern-day Moroccan life, albeit adapted to changing times and needs.

Embroideries accompany every stage of the journey from cradle to grave: the *katfiya* adorns the traditional costume of the new-born baby; the *sebniya* handkerchief covers the bride's hand after the ceremonial application of henna, while the groom is resplendent in tunic, headdress, and gilet. A *shan* headscarf is worn over the hair after bathing, and the deceased are draped in an embroidered shroud for the journey to the afterlife. Cushions known as *mesned* or *mhedda* are scattered on beds and divans or placed on the floor for use as backrests, elbowrests, pillows, or seating. Tablecloths (*mendil*) and smaller squares known as *rzma* have a variety of uses. With their corners knotted together, they make elegant parcels for especially treasured items: the bride's trousseau, gifts from her fiancé, or freshly laundered clothes to take to the hammam.

Large curtains known as *izar* used to be hung in the doorways of rooms opening onto courtyards and enclosed gardens; swollen gently by the evening breeze, their translucent fabric allowed the women of the house to see out, without being seen themselves. In both Chechaouen and Azemmour, large hangings known as *arid* are placed around the bed niche of a newly married couple; in Tétouan, mirrors are adorned with sumptuously embroidered silk bands known as *tenchîfa* to protect against the evil eye.

These embroideries—the product of patience, perseverance, and rigor—never fail to delight, with their subtle nuances, harmonious and rhythmic patterns, powerful compositions, and distinctive styles particular to each individual city. Fez is noted for its delicate monochromatic work, that uses fine geometric and floral motifs, while Rabat's multicolored pieces are clearly distinguishable from the monochromatic, geometric, almost architectural designs of its neighbor, Salé. Tétouan work affords striking similarities with Spanish Muslim embroideries of the fifteenth century but also features the tulips, hyacinths, and wild roses of the Ottoman herbary, themselves a common feature of Algerian embroideries. Azemmour designs draw on the fantastic Byzantine bestiary, and Chechaouen work mingles geometry and floral motifs in shimmering colors reminiscent of manuscript illuminations or mosaics. Meknès embroideries favor abstract, fantastic designs in a multitude of bright, cheerful colors.

Two clear strands of influence are discernible in the embroideries of Morocco. One is Spanish in origin, and the other can be traced to the Balkans. Successive waves of Jewish, Muslim, and Spanish emigrants from Andalusia brought the former to the cities of Fez, Chechaouen, Tétouan, Salé (where two distinctive styles have evolved), Rabat (the city's early work), Azemmour, and Meknès. The latter's influence is discernible in the Fez stitch and the city's so-called *aleuj* embroideries, as practiced by Turkish and Circassian women in the city's harems. These twin traditions are complemented today by the influence of European fabrics, evident in modern Rabat embroidery. But the often-young women who created these pieces were not slaves to tradition. Their works are often highly original, always unique, and feature freely adapted motifs, varied and imaginative compositions, and a fine sense of color. Highly pleasing to the eye, they are also above all a means of communication, an expression of cultural exchange and an eloquent testimony to the lifestyles, emotions, prayers, and dreams of vanished generations of women.

Inspired by these marvelous pieces, Isabelle Denamur has produced a study of great scientific rigor and aesthetic sensitivity—a fitting tribute to their creators, the women of Morocco, past and present.

Marie-France VIVIER
Curator, Maghreb collections, Musée National des Arts d'Afrique et d'Océanie, Paris, and Coordinator of the North African display at the Musée du Quai Branly, Paris.

My contemporaries fall into two camps—those consumed by a passion for Meissen figurines, teddy bears, or little tin soldiers and those (more numerous no doubt and certainly more serene) who have never felt the collector's unquenchable thirst for such things. I sometimes envy the unruffled, orderly, reasonable existence of the latter but am increasingly forced to acknowledge that I have the great good fortune to be counted among the ranks of the former.

At the age of twenty, with Dutch blood in my veins on my mother's side, (two very good reasons for setting out to discover the world) I traveled through Central Asia to the mythical cities of Uzbekistan: Samarkand and Bukhara. Often, after nights huddled beside the flickering hearth of a Mongol yurt, almost deafened by the wind, I seemed to hear the thundering hooves of Ghenghis Khan's hordes, far across the steppe. For a few months I followed, without having planned to, the exact route of the old Silk Road. As I traveled, I became increasingly interested in the traditional textiles and embroideries I came across.

And, thus, I went on to discover Latin America, India, Tibet, Bhutan, and many other countries. But, paradoxically, it was a country far closer to home that exerted the greatest fascination. That country was and still is Morocco.

The emotion I feel when looking at an antique Moroccan textile is difficult to describe. I experience, of course, the soothing pleasure induced by a thing of beauty, but also a dream-like sense of the thread of a story. I feel the presence of another woman who is bent over her sewing frame yet free to lose herself in her work—the only freedom afforded to women of her time, her society. As a woman, I am deeply moved by the sense of escape in such pieces. Down the generations, these *nehza*, these embroiderers of a bygone age, make me feel profoundly connected to this society of women. Sometimes, despite the strictly codified motifs, a careful observer can see a mistake, betrayed by just one stray stitch. These tiny errors are, to me, the most fascinating, the most human aspect of all. One might even fancy that they were made on purpose—as a silent yet eloquent record of past lives and dreams.

Facing Page: *Young Woman Wearing a Fez Kaftan*, 1923, painting by Suzanne Drouet–Reveillaud (1885–1973), private collection.

INTRODUCTION

To date, there has been no systematic study of the highly diverse regional styles of Moroccan embroideries. The present work aims to collect and summarize, as far as possible, the main elements of our scattered knowledge on the subject and to bring it to a wider public in the hope of encouraging interested readers and passionate collectors to make their own discoveries in the field. It may also offer an insight into a valuable heritage—an everyday urban art whose elegance and beauty fire the imagination and whose iconography, once codified, contains precious clues to the complex network of historical and cultural links within which these textiles were created. In its own quiet way, a single motif, stitch, or dye can chronicle a significant slice of Moroccan history.

The intermingling of local and external influences has led to the evolution of a distinctive set of motifs and decorative designs, albeit largely influenced by the styles of Muslim Spain. The civilizations of Morocco and the Iberian peninsula were closely linked for nearly one thousand years, from the eighth to the seventeenth centuries. However, the influence of Spanish Muslim culture in Morocco declined after 1610, when the Moors from Andalusia were increasingly being assimilated into local society and culture.

Spain and the Maghreb first encountered one another under the conquering Almoravids. By the end of the eleventh century, these Saharan nomads, ancestors of present-day Tuaregs, controlled an empire encompassing southern Spain and the western Berber territories. The Almoravids fostered close and long-lasting cultural links, notably through significant movements of population. Most of the main attacks on Spain were led by the Moroccan Berbers, who subsequently returned to settle in the cities of northern Morocco and whose movements and influence defined the character of western Islamic culture for centuries to come.

The Almohads were mountain-dwellers from the Atlas Mountains, whose empire succeeded that of the Almoravids and encompassed Andalusia and the whole of North Africa. However, they were finally driven out of Spain in the seventeenth century by the Christian Reconquista. Under their influence, the institutions, arts, and skills of Muslim Spain gradually took hold in cities throughout the Maghreb; at the same time, the ornate splendor of Spanish Muslim decorative arts gave way to a more sober, classical style. Purity of line then became the overriding concern of Andalusian craftsmen and architects.

The decorative arts in Morocco spring from two distinct but parallel origins whose paths cross only rarely. Work produced by the Berbers and almost all other Arabized tribes, virtually the whole of rural Morocco, is rustic in character and technically unsophisticated. The designs are characterized by a powerful stylistic coherence: geometric, rectilinear shapes common to all regions but with numerous local variations within the patterns themselves.

Berber art is indigenous not only to Morocco but also to North Africa as a whole. As such, a close study will offer an insight into the region's oldest traditions—perhaps even a glimpse of its deepest soul. The second strand of influence can be traced back to the Almoravids and the Almohads. These two dynasties (and particularly that of the Almohads) grew and developed on Morocco's home soil and were enriched by conquest. The Maghrebi, who embraced Spanish Muslim art, eventually became its major producers. In this way, the urban Hispanic-Moorish style evolved into the "official" art of Morocco, distinct from, yet significantly influenced by, the folk art of the Berber tribes.

Geometric elements in Berber art are central to the Hispanic-Moorish decoration. Berber geometry is characterized by lively, bold patterns congruent with the logic of the overall design, a design that incorporates both straight lines and curves. The intertwining, interpenetrating curves typical of Arab art are in total contrast to the vigorous, rhythmic, symmetrical lines of the Berber style. The meeting of these traditions gave rise to the local urban art of the Maghreb, which was thus partly Oriental and partly Berber.

Embroidered decoration is essentially floral, always highly stylized, and profusely applied but rigorously structured. Hispanic-Moorish art is never innovative; rather, it is gradually evolving and being refined within a certain stylistic repertory. The result is a sophisticated mix of floral and geometric motifs. Unhindered by the need to create a faithful reproduction of nature, the artist is free to concentrate on the purely decorative. Abstraction and stylization reign supreme; there is no attempt at a realistic representation of form. Yet the designs and patterns encapsulate the very essence of the living world, namely movement.

The rich diversity of Moroccan embroideries is also derived partially from Balkan sources. This is particularly true of *aleuj* work and the Fez stitch, imported by the Turkish and Circassian women in the Fezzi harems.

Any study of Moroccan embroideries should, then, acknowledge and identify the numerous local and external influences discernible in their designs and motifs. We should also acknowledge the central importance of embroidery to Moroccan domestic and social life. In the past, the ownership of sumptuous embroideries conferred a particular prestige. High-ranking women adorned themselves with embroidered garments and displayed fine pieces of work in their homes. Those who did not own such items were considered poor. This state of affairs has considerably altered today.

At the time of Moroccan independence in 1956, the majority of women still decorated their homes with fine embroideries. These days, traditional embroidered cushions have been replaced in most homes by modern ones. The marvelous embroidered textiles that once spoke so eloquently of the hopes and fears of their young creators have now become old-fashioned—a radical turnabout in just four decades, one which holds little hope for the future of Moroccan embroidery. Traditional examples still in existence are both spectacular works of art and precious testament to age-old local tradition.

Embroidery: A Woman's Art

MA'ALLEMA, MUHTASIB, CHELLIGA...

The art of embroidery enjoyed great popularity in Morocco until the first third of the nineteenth century. The original works that have come down to us from this period show great finesse and taste, testifying to their important role in Moroccan society and life.

EMBROIDERY: A WOMAN'S ART

MOROCCAN TEXTILE EMBROIDERY

The art of embroidery enjoyed great popularity in Morocco until the first third of the nineteenth century. The original works that have come down to us from this period show great finesse and taste, testifying to their important role in Moroccan society and life.

Skillful embroidery teachers, the *ma'allemat* (the feminine of *ma'allem*, or "master craftsman"), initiated Moroccan girls into the secrets of their art from an early age. The teachers visited the homes of middle-class families or held classes for girls from poorer families in their own workshops. Christiane Brunot-David notes that at four months, a girl is seated in a child's chair, "and a needle, thimble, and silk thread are placed in her hands, so that she might become an accomplished embroideress. [The ceremony] clearly demonstrates the prestige of embroidery in urban society in Morocco."

Up until the mid-twentieth century, the practice of embroidery provided entertainment and escape for wellborn young girls and women, who rarely left their homes. The girls worked on their own bridal trousseaux, household articles, and traditional items of costume—both everyday clothing and ceremonial wear.

Both wealthy and more modest urban interiors featured numerous embroidered items, such as cushions, the use of which was very widespread. Covered in silk or brocade, decorated with embroidery, they were displayed at the head and foot of a bed or divan and used as backrests, elbowrests, pillows, and seats. Traditional embroidered tablecloths and napkins were also commonly used up until the first third of the twentieth century, while beds were decorated with embroidered accessories in almost all Moroccan towns. All were indispensable, important accoutrements in the daily life of the urban household.

In Tétouan, for important ceremonies or weddings, long veils embroidered at each end were hung from mirrors. A young girl's trousseau also included large bathing scarves, sumptuously decorated trouser sashes, shawls, and kerchiefs of various sizes.

APPRENTICESHIP AND PROFESSION

MOROCCAN TEXTILE EMBROIDERY

As the studies of embroidery in Fez carried out by Anne-Marie Goichon and Jean-Pierre Bernes have shown, the apprenticeship and work of the embroiderers were highly organized. From a very early age, girls were introduced to the art of embroidery at the home of a woman teacher—the head of her own workshop—known as the *ma'allema*. As in Tétouan, girls in Fez were taught free of charge, but, in Rabat, their apprenticeship had to be paid. When a girl completed her training, a sample of her work was kept by the *ma'allema*, and she went on to produce work for her teacher's clients.

The teacher accepted as many pupils as she had room for but instructed them in small groups of a dozen or so, thereby ensuring her closest attention to their work and progress. The girls also worked on items for themselves and their families, such as medium-sized cushions, long bands of mattress trimming, and bolsters. Items begun at the teacher's workshop were finished at home in the evening. Up until the mid-twentieth century, fathers in Fez would purchase their daughters' sewing frames, fabrics, and silks. When the daughter married, the sums demanded for her dowry varied considerably according to the quantity of her embroideries. Parents whose daughters had not been taught embroidery would order items for the dowry from a *ma'allema*, which the bride would then take to her new home.

Women of all classes, privileged and poor alike, worked as embroiderers in Morocco. Many poorer women preferred embroidery to other more menial tasks. Wives and mothers would often supplement their husbands' irregular incomes by taking on embroidery work, while middle-class or noble women often sewed in secret at home, selling their pieces anonymously in order to avoid the stigma of having been paid for their work, which was incompatible with their social status.

In addition to the embroidery commissions received from the *ma'allema*, some women embroidered household items and clothing in the hope of selling them for profit. Such items were not produced to order, and the embroiderer provided her own materials. To sell them, she had to use the services of an intermediary—a street crier, shopkeeper, or another woman less well off than herself. Work produced for this highly localized market was generally rather mediocre; well-executed pieces were rare; the fabrics and silks were of inferior quality, and the choice of colors often betrayed a lack of taste. These pieces were produced for a poorer clientele who, unable to embroider the items themselves, bought them at the market.

Other women preferred to work at home for European clients who paid generously and did not expect them to provide their own materials. In this case, there was a clear distinction between the quality of work produced for shops and that done to order for individual clients.

In Fez, embroiderers, unlike the city's craftsmen, never organized themselves into a formal, structured guild. They were thus able to work from home and, unlike other craftspeople, they paid no tax. While the official craft guilds of Fez were organized into separate districts, each practicing a particular trade, embroiderers were to be found in every street of the city's medina or old town.

The commercial exploitation of embroidery brought considerable benefits to the less wealthy families involved, but it also led to a decline in quality in an art form that is unforgiving of mediocrity.

School of Embroidery in Morocco, 1927, Edouard Brindeau de Jarny (Paris, 1867–1947), private collection.

Above: *Rzma* (square for making a bundle), Rabat, nineteenth century, silk embroidery on cotton, running stitch, back stitch, feather stitch, length 4 ft. 9 in. (150 cm), width 4 ft. 7 in. (144 cm), private collection.
Facing page: *Dar Jamaï,* living room, Fez, anonymous, c. 1930, private collection.

Christiane Brunot-David's detailed study of embroidery in Rabat reveals much about the role of the *ma'allema*. Here, the *ma'allema* never taught pupils in her own home but ran her school and workshop from the *dar msallema* (the embroiderer's house), a veritable center of activity in its own right and a focus for the concerns of her apprentices and their parents. *Ma'allemat* came from a wide range of backgrounds, although never from the very poorest or wealthiest, and were professionals rather than artists, motivated less by an instinctive love of the medium or the work than by a desire to establish themselves and earn a living from their talents. Once their businesses and incomes were established, they were often eagerly courted by men from more modest backgrounds. Some married wealthy men—or men who later became so—and gave up their work.

A teacher who was also skilled in the drawing of embroidery designs and patterns, a *ma'allema ressama*, had a clear advantage over women whose knowledge was limited to stitching and who embroidered for pleasure. The *ma'allema ressama* could earn significant sums from the sale of her designs and did not depend entirely on teaching for her living. She would also supervise the production of work to order, providing other women with designs to embroider. Her fees were based on the complexity of the design, the nature and fabric of the item to be decorated, and the weight and colors of the silks used. Sometimes the client herself supplied the materials. Multicolored work was more costly than monochromatic, and work on delicate fabrics such as tulle or muslin fetched a higher price than work on linen or cotton. With no salaried employees of her own, creating designs and supervising pieces to order were highly profitable activities for the *ma'allema ressama*.

With no officially agreed rates, each *ma'allema ressama* was free to set her own, although this was sometimes a source of conflict with her embroiderers and clients. In the absence of a formal guild, disputes were arbitrated by the *muhtasib* (market inspector). When an amicable solution could not be found, the *muhtasib* sometimes asked one or two other trusted embroiderers to give their opinion on the value of the work in question.

Without the benefit of a formal price structure, families often haggled over the cost of an apprenticeship. When setting her fees, the *ma'allema* took account of the wealth or otherwise of her pupil's family before agreeing a monthly sum with the girl's mother, payable throughout the apprenticeship. In Rabat, each apprentice paid according to her means, but no one was taught free of charge. Christiane Brunot-David notes that the pupil's "artistic induction is seen as an almost magical, arcane initiation which demands and deserves payment." Other expenses, such as the purchase of straw mats and drinking jars for the girls' comfort, were sometimes added to the monthly fee.

Samplers known as *chelliga* were used as teaching tools to present examples of the various stitches to be mastered in the workshop by the pupil over the course of her apprenticeship. These samples generally took the form of a medium-sized piece of everyday fabric, with each motif executed in a different color of cotton thread—red, yellow, blue, black, or green. Silk thread was not normally used. As Marie-France Vivier observed: "The apprenticeship concludes with the production of a sampler—a kind of graduation diploma and an invaluable repertory of stitches and motifs whose organization and presentation testify to the *ma'allema*'s qualities as a teacher."

Traditionally, the *ma'allema* was presented with bread and cakes at her pupils' family celebrations. On religious holidays, each pupil offered her mistress a further small gift. These small rituals reinforced social ties and created a positive, friendly environment within the *dar msallema*. This approach to communal endeavors is typical of Islamic societies.

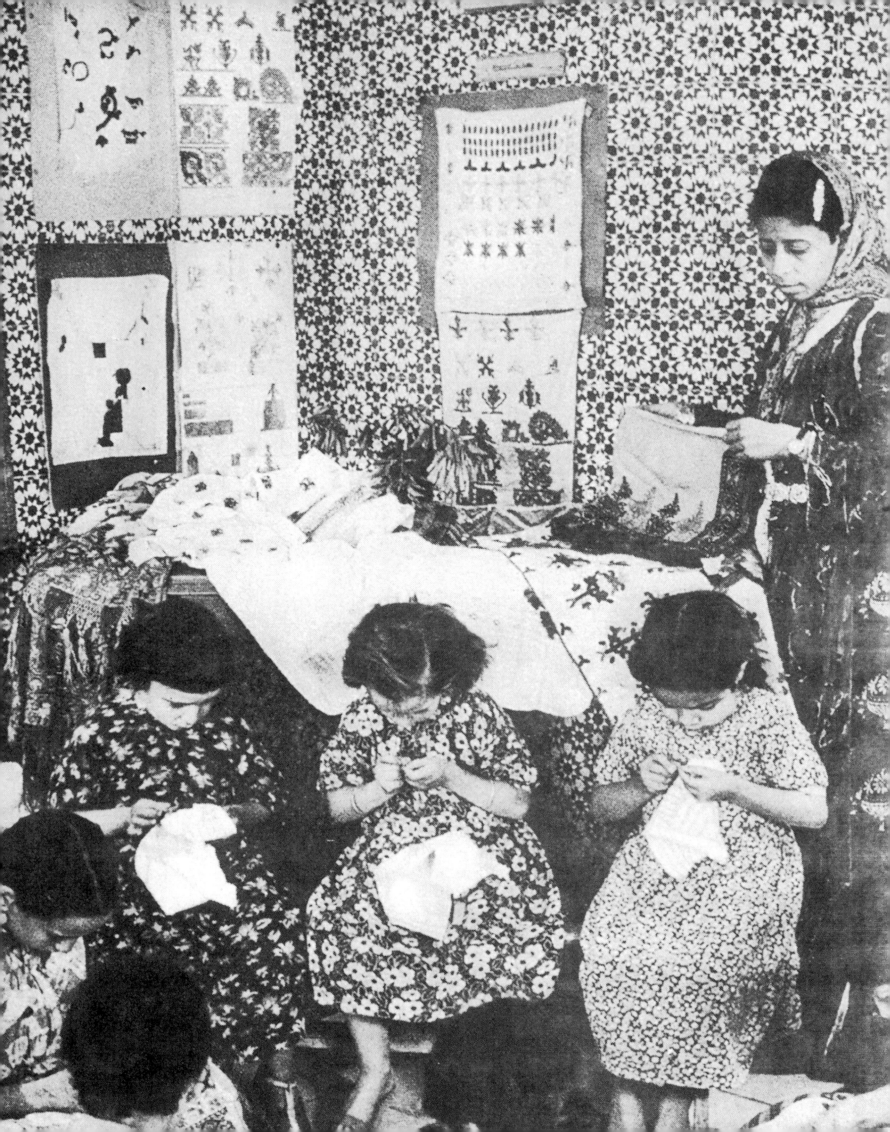

Facing page and above: *Chelliga* (sampler), silk embroidery on cotton, nineteenth century, length 28 in. (71 cm), width 16 in. (41 cm), private collection.

E mbroidery was still a flourishing, living art in the mid-nineteenth century, practiced professionally and enjoyed socially by a great many women from both wealthy and poorer levels of society.

Writing in the mid-1970s, Jean-Pierre Bernes noted that although it was almost impossible to estimate their number, reliable accounts indicated that as late as 1930, some 2,500 *ma'allemat* still specialized in gold-thread embroidery in Fez alone, with an additional 2,000 artisans working in silk thread.

But we must ask ourselves what is the role of embroidery in Moroccan society today? Its value in the eyes of many women has considerably altered. It is first and foremost a social language, and its function and evolving role are best observed in the home or workshop, where the embroideries them-selves are produced.

Today, Moroccan clothing and domestic interiors are clearly strongly influenced by Western styles. Since Moroccan independence from France in 1956, the form and function of garments and household items have become, slowly but surely, increasingly Westernized. The demise of the curtain is particularly significant: once used to conceal the women of the house, it is now defunct. And inevitably, young girls today no longer aspire to become embroiderers. They attend school, and prefer to spend their free time on other, more contemporary, pursuits.

As in so many other countries, regional lifestyles, and particularities within Morocco have become increasingly homogenized, too, with inevitable consequences for the diversity of traditional decorative arts. This is particularly true of embroidery, which was traditionally one of the most regionally distinctive and idiosyncratic forms of artistic expression. The quality of an embroidered item was determined by the personality, character, and skill of one woman, and by her personal preferences, for a particular type of linen or silk, a stitch, a motif.

In bygone days, a sumptuous bourgeois interior, richly decorated with embroideries, was a badge of great distinction. Today's interiors are more likely to take their cue from Western styles, however, and are increasingly homogenous.

There are still a handful of women who strive to preserve their heritage, and who keep a few antique pieces to show to their daughters or friends, but it is certain, however, that modern living, modern clothes, and modern tastes are putting an end to this difficult, marvelous art.

But while these exceptional pieces have lost their original social function, they can still, undoubtedly, be appreciated for their extraordinary aesthetic qualities.

Page 34: *Shan* (shawl), Fez, early-nineteenth century, monochromatic silk embroidery on embroidered cotton gauze, length 6 ft. 7 in. (204 cm), width 24 in. (60 cm), private collection.
Page 35: *Young Woman Wearing an Embroidered Shan* [shawl], c. 1934–39, photograph by Jean Besancenot (France, 1902–1992), Institut du Monde Arabe, Paris.

n Morocco, imported European fabric, almost always white, was used as the base fabric for embroidery. Cotton was the commonest fabric, but occasionally linen was used and also, on rare occasions, silk. Traditionally, tussore, crêpe-de-Chine, Moroccan crêpe, or challis were never used in work for the local market. These fabrics were reserved for European clients and the resulting place mats, cushions, and shawls are of considerable artistic value.

As a general rule, Moroccan embroiderers have paid little attention to the base fabric for their work. However, a new generation of apprentices now being taught in the country's schools is learning the importance of the choice of fabric and color for the support. Satin is no longer used, except in Tétouan, as its brilliance makes the embroidered motifs look dull. Overly harsh white fabrics are also out of favor, as they tend to diminish the colors used in the embroidery. Some new fabrics have been adopted for the local market, including challis and tussore silk, favored for their matt texture and discreet colors, enabling the embroiderers to harmonize the colors of the base fabric with those used in the embroidery and, thus, creating an impression of relief.

Generally silk thread is used, which is bought rolled onto a piece of reed. The best grade comes from India, hence its local name *hrir hindi* (Indian silk). Another, an inferior thread, is used for joining separate pieces together, buttons, trimmings, and (rarely) embroidery. For reasons of cost, embroiderers also use overly shiny artificial silk, known as *hrir sabra* ("aloe silk") or simply *jdijdi* ("new type"). When the silks used are not ready-dyed, the local dyer is responsible for ensuring the colors are fast. Morocco's indigenous silk industry, which once produced thread of very high quality and should have prospered, was in fact undermined by the incompetence of Moroccan dyers. Today, ready-dyed silks are all imported from Europe.

During their early training, apprentice embroiderers use pearl cotton and, more recently, artificial silk rather than silk thread. The rest of their equipment is simple in the extreme sense, consisting of nothing more than needles of various sizes (imported from Europe), a thimble, and a small cushion to which the work in progress is pinned. In Fez, sewing frames—an adjustable wooden frame mounted on four legs—are used. The largest needles, with a long, wide eye, are used to embroider curtains. Needles can be bought in packets, but young apprentices can also buy them individually. Some embroideries are executed using double, triple, or even quadruple skeins of thread. In the past, this used to be an important consideration for the embroiderer, when the commercial value of her work was determined by the quantity of silk used. Thus the piece to be embroidered would be weighed before she began work, and after she had finished. The thimbles are also imported from Europe, and are identical to those used in the couture houses of Paris.

In place of a sewing frame (used only in Fez), the embroiderer places a small cushion on her knees. The cushion is stuffed with wool or straw, depending on her family's means, and covered with coarse cotton. The work in hand is held in place on the cushion with the aid of pins and tacking on the three sides furthest from the embroiderer herself. As she works, she slips her hand beneath the fourth side.

CREATING AND EXECUTING A DESIGN
MOROCCAN TEXTILE EMBROIDERY

When it is necessary, a trained *ma'-allema* will draw her design in pencil, freehand and with great confidence, without the use of transfers or tracing paper, directly onto the fabric, which is spread out on a table or a piece of cardboard resting on the knees. Tétouan embroiderers buy items ready-drawn in this way. In Fez, stamps are used for the designs of certain *aleuj* pieces, but this practice has been little studied. In Rabat, on the other hand, the designs are drawn freehand by the individual embroiderers themselves, their vigorous motifs dictated by the imagination, albeit within the bounds of a firmly established style. This approach is quicker and less restrictive than that adopted in Fez, Salé, and Meknès, where the designs are based on counted threads, but the technique demands considerable dexterity and skill. The results are generally good, however. On unfinished antique pieces, preparatory drawings are sometimes visible.

The type of stitch used is an indication of the town in which a piece of embroidery was made, although some pieces feature different types. The quality of the stitch can be a fair indicator of its age. Jeanne Jouin notes: "The cross stitch is used occasionally for isolated motifs in the embroideries of Salé and Azemmour. Lines are traced, and larger areas filled in, with a simple plaited stitch and a running stitch. The so-called "Old Salé" embroideries and early examples from Fez are worked in a running stitch and a double-sided brick stitch. All of these stitches are found in the highly eclectic embroideries of Meknès. The motifs of *aleuj* work are filled with an oblique, overlapping *petit point*, the use of which has long since died out in Morocco. Modern Rabat embroidery is worked in a satin stitch. Old Rabat work employs a broad, flat scalloped stitch, and a broad plaited stitch for the edges of motifs; contours are finished with picot."

The use of a number of additional stitches—such as a lockstitch, a feather stitch from Salé, and a star stitch from Fez—has also spread throughout all regions. Most of the motifs used in Moroccan embroidery are based on counted-thread work—and for good reason, since this is by far the safest way to produce excellent, everyday pieces, facilitating the work of even the most inept seamstress. Rabat and Tétouan embroideries, as well as *aleuj* work, require an underdrawing.

The double-sided, reversible embroideries of Fez are more complex. The needlework needs to be planned so that the threads of the ground that are left blank in one direction are covered on the return. This avoids unnecessary maneuvers. Once the basic technique has been mastered, the work becomes rather mechanical.

All of these stitches result in dense, closely worked areas of embroidery. The use of thick, luxuriant silks gives a characteristically rich, sumptuous finish. Other stitches, like the running stitch, chain stitch, and plaited stitch, are only used for secondary ornamental features. While often found with numerous variations in older work, they are rarely seen in modern, everyday pieces.

Facing page: *Young Woman in an Embroidered Turban*, c. 1934–39, photograph by Jean Besancenot (1902–1992), Institut du Monde Arabe, Paris.

The range, variety, and durability of the embroiderer's color palette depend on the dye techniques used for the silks. Silks chemically dyed in Europe offer a huge range of colors of varying quality. In Fez, embroiderers can obtain silks dyed in the traditional way but with chemical colors. The local, indigenous dyeing industry also supplies silks dyed using traditional natural vegetable or animal pigments.

The enlightened *ma'allema* is a discerning customer who knows that only natural vegetable or animal dyes will produce shimmering, durable colors and tones. She knows, too, that indigenous dyes will only be absorbed effectively on high-quality silks such as white *hindi*. Nonetheless, artificial silks with bright, aggressive aniline-based colors are inevitably popular among poorer, less discerning urban embroiderers, who are drawn to cheap, poor-quality European goods. This is doubly regrettable in view of the fact that aniline-based colors are short-lived and fade quickly when washed or exposed to sunlight. Good-quality chemical and vegetable dyes are becoming available at comparable prices, but their use requires specialist knowledge and equipment not possessed by most indigenous dyers. Embroiderers can purchase chemically dyed silks from a silk merchant, or silks colored with vegetable dyes direct from a local dyer. As Christiane Brunot-David explains, these factors have enabled the indigenous dyeing industry to survive, although it is far from enjoying a monopoly.

Indigenous dyers dye both silk and wool using identical processes and materials. Seven basic raw materials are used. Indigo comes in the form of a blue powder obtained from the fermentation of indigo plants from Egypt, India, or Java. Madder grows wild around Marrakech and produces a range of tones from prawn-pink to garnet. Cochineal, made from the dried, powdered bodies of insects and produced mostly in Spain, yields brighter reds. Weld, also known as yellow weed or dyer's weed, produces a pale yellow and is common in Morocco. Another North African plant, daphne, gives a more greenish yellow. Henna, costly and hence little used, is powder obtained from the leaves and twigs from the henna shrub (*Lawsonia inermis*). It produces a range of colors from bright yellow through to deep rust reds, auburn, or purplish black. Pomegranate bark gives a black of varying strength, depending on the dye used.

These ingredients cover the basic colors. The length of time for which the silk is immersed in the dye bath determines their strength. Colors are mixed by immersing the silk in two or three different baths in succession, giving an even richer variety of tints and tones. The dyer will also sometimes add a very small amount of chemical dye. This provides an added nuance but does nothing to detract from the brilliance and strength of the natural colors. Alum, which does not affect the tone of the colors, is the only mordant that is used.

The choice and use of colors in embroidered designs are influenced by fashion. Colors that are highly prized today were little used or unknown in the past. The dominant color of antique embroideries is dark blue, while yellow and red are often used in more modern pieces. Popular taste today clearly favors brighter, louder colors, while pieces commissioned through the *ma'allema* are still characterized by the traditional, more subtle nuances of color and tone described earlier.

With the exception of Tétouan pieces, all Moroccan embroideries are worked on an off-white ground that serves to enhance the exceptional brilliance of the embroidered decorations. The palette used ranges from the monochromatic embroideries of the past to the multicolored designs of recent work. The number and range of colors used depends entirely on personal taste. It is for this reason that *ma'allemat* favor natural dyes, which are more forgiving of the sometimes injudicious color combinations chosen by inexperienced pupils. As Christiane Brunot-David points out, the embroidery mistress often provides harmoniously colored antique embroideries as models for her pupils. The resulting reproductions are sold to discerning European clients, proving highly profitable. "In this way, the girls assimilate and understand the mercantile value of aesthetically beautiful work."

DECORATING THE UTILITARIAN
MOROCCAN TEXTILE EMBROIDERY

The use of embroiderery in Morocco is generally restricted to the decoration of utilitarian objects. Embroidered pieces are never hung in a frame like a picture in the Western manner. The motifs chosen should never interfere with the object's utilitarian function; ideally, they should enhance it. An embroidered border along the bottom of a fine curtain will ensure that it hangs better. On napkins or towels, it can help prevent the corners from fraying. A riot of embroidered trimmings on mattresses and divans is highly pleasing to the eye and does not detract from their comfort.

In Tétouan, during the forty-day honeymoon period following a wedding, mirrors in the nuptial chamber are covered with made-to-measure veils known as *tenchîfa* to guard against the evil eye. The walls are decked with hangings known as *ajar*, hung horizontally, and the bed may be covered with an *ajara* spread; brilliant embroidered silk cushions (*mhâïd*) complete the scheme. In Tétouan, embroideries are found only on household items and furnishings.

In Chechaouen, on ceremonial occasions long bands known as *arid* are hung from the shelf framing across the bed niches. These bands are also used to cover storage chests. Two pieces may also be sewn along the sides of a large piece of linen to form a bedcover.

In Fez, a small square napkin known as a *gelsa* marks the place of honor reserved for guests on the reception-room divan. The *telmîta* (plural *tlâmet*) is a long decorative band sewn around the edges of mattresses. The *medersa*, or cushion, is used as a pillow at night, and as a backrest, seat, or elbow-rest during the waking hours. Bedroom accoutrements also include a number of large cushions featuring closely worked, dense areas of embroidery.

Elegant ladies wear embroidered sashes (*tekka*) and stockings (*merbet*) beneath their caftans; embroidered accessories may include handkerchiefs (*mherma*), scarves (*derra*), and bath shawls (*shan*). Richly embroidered tablecloths known as *mendil* are found in Meknès (the same word is also used to describe handcloths, tray cloths, and children's veils). The *mendil* is also used to wrap a woman's change of clothes on visits to the hammam.

Rabat is noted for its love of show and sumptuous furnishings. During festivals, the city's inhabitants deck their doorframes with large, heavily embroidered curtains (*izar*). Divans in elegant reception rooms are decked with cushions, pillows, bolsters, valances, and mats. Embroidery in Rabat is used mainly for large, sumptuous furnishings, but embroidered clothes and layette articles are also found.

In Salé, domestic interiors are decorated with sumptuous curtains, door hangings, and cushions.

Facing page: *Izar* (door hanging), Rabat, nineteenth century, polychromatic silk floss embroidery on embroidered tulle, length 10 ft. (320 cm), width 5 ft. 8 in. (176 cm), private collection.

DECORATING THE UTILITARIAN
MOROCCAN TEXTILE EMBROIDERY

In Azemmour, embroidery is found only on strips of ecru-colored canvas used to decorate the edges of silk hangings and mattresses. In towns where such luxuries are the preserve of only a few families, they are readily hired out or loaned to others for family celebrations.

As a general rule, then, embroidery is used in Morocco solely for the purpose of decorating useful items such as household furnishings and ladies' toilet accessories. The Moroccan embroiderer never forgets the practical purpose of the item she decorates. Decoration is the servant of practicality, not its master.

Facing page: *Preparations for the Wedding of the Daughter of the Cherif in Tangiers*, painting by José Tapiro y Bara (1830–1913), private collection.

The Kingdom of Embroidery

AAJARA, TENCHÎFA, ARID, CHAN

A study of Moroccan embroidery takes us, then, on an imaginary journey from Tétouan to Chechaouen, whose styles are closely similar, from Fez to Meknès, from Rabat to Salé, and on to Azemmour.

THE KINGDOM OF EMBROIDERY

MOROCCAN TEXTILE EMBROIDERY

Situated at the northwestern tip of Africa, Morocco possesses an extensive coastline that embraces the Mediterranean to the north and the Atlantic to the west. It is separated from Spain—but only just—by the Strait of Gibraltar. Its eastern frontier is shared, along virtually its entire length, with Algeria.

Embroidery in Morocco was first practiced in the country's northern towns and is essentially an urban art form. It is characterized by no fewer than seven distinct styles, each identified by the name of its town of origin.

A study of Moroccan embroidery takes us then on an imaginary journey from Tétouan to Chechaouen, both of whose styles are closely similar, from Fez to

Meknès, from Rabat to Salé and on to Azemmour. Almost every town or city has its own distinctive colors, stitches, and technique and its own ornamental vocabulary, based on abstract motifs, or figures derived from the animal and plant worlds. As Jeanne Jouin has observed: "Moroccan art makes no attempt to imitate the natural world, and the presence of figurative representations, however stylized, almost always indicates a foreign influence. Embroidery is no exception. Moroccan embroiderers do not seek to imitate nature. Their decorations consist entirely of either abstract motifs or stylized derivations."

The abstract elements seen in Tétouan and Chechaouen embroideries are typical of the basic

decorative vocabulary underpinning embroidery styles throughout Morocco. They are essentially rectilinear, geometric, simple, and legible; Moroccan embroiderers show little inclination for the curvaceous designs used in other branches of the decorative arts and disdain the tracery favored in Hispanic-Moorish art. Common geometric motifs include crosses, stars, lattices, chevrons, and serrations. Fez embroideries are characterized by the use of broken lines, diamond shapes, and stars, giving them an austere but powerful and distinguished appearance. The elongated hexagons used in Salé are softer in character, while most Tétouan designs are based on a square. Decorative inscriptions are rare but sometimes seen in Tétouan and Chechaouen work.

Motifs derived from leaves and flowers are equally important in Moroccan embroideries. These are often highly original and more clearly identifiable with a particular city or region than their geometric counterparts. A flower or plant motif on a curtain in Fez will be quite unlike one from Tétouan, Salé, or Rabat.

As Jeanne Jouin has noted: "The representations of living creatures, albeit highly stylized, which we find in Azemmour embroideries, are an anomaly in Morocco as a whole. Seemingly, these rare pieces were in fact produced by Jewish women." Writing in the 1960s and 1970s, Martha Guérard, too, was surprised to find novel "representations of figures" in certain works. Other commentators have examined the traditional ban in Islam on representations of living creatures. André Goldenburg notes that the only source for this is the Hadith—the body of often-corrupted and misreported traditions relating to the sayings of the prophet Mohammed. There is, indeed, nothing in the Koran to support this ban. André Paccard confirms this view, adding that the precepts expressed in the Hadith were probably not spoken by the Prophet himself but written down by learned Islamic clerics in the ninth century. "Nonetheless," he observes, "the ban remains sacrosanct in the Islamic world today; it was respected in the interiors of religious buildings from the faith's earliest beginnings and was quickly applied to all other art forms."

Page 47: *Ladies' Outing*, c. 1934–39, photograph by Jean Besancenot (1902–1992), private collection.
Facing page: *Harem at Rest*, Marrakech, 1943, painting by Jacques Majorelle (1886–1962), private collection.

TÉTOUAN

HISPANIC-MOORISH TRACES

Tétouan pieces are worked on fine fabrics such as challis or fine-grade linen. Older pieces conserve the latter's natural colors (ivory or beige-gray), while more recent embroideries are worked on colored silk, which is frequently dyed a bright flame yellow or old gold, intense raspberry red, saturated sky blue, vivid bottle green, or shocking violet.

TÉTOUAN

I n her interesting study of Moroccan embroideries, Martha Guérard notes: "In Tétouan, the art of embroidery often seems to have achieved perfection." Numerous eyewitness accounts describe the past luxury and refinement of the city's wealthier homes; Tétouan was also renowned for the finesse of its other traditional arts—weaving, *zellige* work (enameled mosaics, using a different technique from that seen in Fez, and still a local specialty), and leatherwork. The city's craft schools and embroidery workshops were justly famous—the latter producing distinctive work of great originality.

Described by the poets as "Granada's daughter," Tétouan was founded by the Marinids in the early-fourteenth century. The city was a military base, intended to quell the rebellious tribespeople of Rif, but it soon became the haunt of pirates and was completely destroyed by Henri II of Castille in 1399. The fall of the kingdom of Granada in 1492 marked the rebirth of Tétouan, which was quickly settled by refugee Spanish Jews, along with Muslims from Cadiz, Granada, Baeza, and Almería (already celebrated for its fabrics). The city prospered and became an active center for trade and, once again,

Page 51: *Decorative detail from a tenchîfa* (mirror veil), Tétouan, early-nineteenth century, natural polychromatic silk embroidery on natural sand-colored silk, running stitch, back stitch and brick stitch, length 14 ft. (440 cm), width 24 in. (61 cm), private collection.

piracy. Tétouan was the last stronghold and kingdom of Muslim Spain to fall to the Christians. The Spanish set out to destroy the slave trade—a major source of wealth for the pirates of Tétouan. Piracy ceased, but legal commerce suffered, too. As Morocco's principal gateway to Europe, Tétouan prospered anew under the reign of Moulay Ismail (1672–1727) and developed important new commercial links with the West. As a result, the city became Morocco's diplomatic capital from the eighteenth century onward.

In the medieval casbahs of Tétouan and Chechaouen, comparable in architecture to the Moorish fortresses of Spain, Andalusian exiles kept alive the tradition of Hispanic-Moorish embroidery, itself of Coptic and Oriental origin.

The city's Andalusian heritage has profoundly influenced every aspect of Tétouan life—from cooking to music, jewelry, and embroidery. Nasrid and Hispanic-Moorish motifs (the former being the last Arab dynasty in Spain) survive in Tétouan embroideries, and fine examples can be seen in the museum of ethnography at Bâb Oukla. A small community of families from Algiers also settled in the city, bringing with them two styles of Turkish-inspired embroidery. Today, the Turkish origins of Tétouan embroidery are widely accepted. Indeed, Jean Hainault and Henri Terrasse assert that Moroccan embroidery styles are almost all derived from the various regions of the former Turkish empire: Asia Minor, Transcaucasia, and the Balkans. The brilliant embroideries of both Turkey and Tétouan are indeed characterized by the same overlapping double-back stitch, the same floral motifs, and the same sumptuous colors.

Jeanne Jouin, however, states that the Turkish embroidery styles brought to Tétouan by the former rulers of Algiers (the Turks) are only distantly related to the city's indigenous style. The Turko-Algerian embroideries were, in fact, far removed from their Balkan antecedents, while the local styles came to resemble the latter to a greater and greater extent. "This aesthetic homecoming may," Jouin suggests, "have been influenced by the imports of Levantine goods and workers to Tétouan." Turkish cultural influences in the Maghreb were undoubtedly augmented by the annexation of Libya, Tunisia, and Algeria to the Ottoman empire in 1535.

While confirming that Turkish and other textiles were indeed introduced to the Maghreb during the three centuries of Turkish occupation, Paul Vandenbroeck questions the depth of their influence on the clearly Oriental stylistic traditions of Fez, Meknès, Rabat, and other Moroccan cities, which never came under Turkish domination. "The art-historical obsession with stylistic influence does not contribute to our understanding of traditional styles in urban textiles," he insists.

Facing page: *Wedding Ceremony in Tétouan*, c. 1900, anonymous, Indianapolis Museum of Art.

Certain pieces, however, clearly demonstrate Turkish influence, notably a bursa velvet, used as a horse's saddle blanket, woven sometime between 1550 and 1650 and in the collection of the Museum of Islamic Art in Cairo (page 57). From the carpet's red ground and gold-lamé decoration, a new floral design emerges, clearly inspired by Turkish models in the purist Ottoman style created in the mid-sixteenth century during the reign of Suleyman. It features characteristic Ottoman flowers, namely the car-nation, tulip, hyacinth, and wild rose, the latter with its distinctive serrated leaves. As such, the sixteenth-century horse cover documents the hitherto rather mysterious genesis of Tétouan embroidery's distinctive motifs.

Often depicted in profile, the carnation is shown in full bloom, flanked by a calyx composed of diverse elements. It is most often seen decorating *tenchîfa*, or mirror hangings. Stylized, but still clearly recognizable, the hyacinth and wild rose are depicted from the front, often ringed by several annuli. They are found on *tenchîfa*, curtains, cushions and tablecloths. The wild-rose leaves, with their strongly serrated edges, are a favorite motif in the Tétouan repertory and often resemble, in their stylized form, a horseshoe or sawtooth shape, depending on whether they are depicted frontally or from the side. The wild-rose leaf motif contains an ovoid form (a stylized pomegranate)

that is often seen in textiles and embroideries from both Asia Minor and Hungary. Trefoils and florets are found in all compositions.

Thick and spiny, resembling the trunk of a powerful tree, the stem, loaded with flowers and fruit, is a striking feature of the designs adorning *tenchîfa*, cushions, and mats. The tulip, often embroidered on mirror hangings, is robust and stylized, unlike its fine, etiolated counterpart in Turkish work.

Unlike the majority of Moroccan embroideries, Tétouan stitches are worked on fine fabrics such as challis or fine-grade linen. Older pieces conserve the latter's natural colors (ivory or beige-gray), while more recent embroideries are worked on colored silk, which is frequently dyed a bright flame yellow or old gold, intense raspberry red, saturated sky blue, vivid bottle green, or shocking violet. Occasionally, darker colors are used.

A sumptuous mix of fine, multicolored, naturally dyed silks adds to the effect of the work, characterized by the effective use of contrasting bold and pale colors and tones. The basic design is characterized by larger shapes, picked out in bold colors, and smaller, secondary elements in softer shades. A variety of filling stitches are used for the main elements, including brick stitch, running stitch and occasionally darning stitch. The work is not

Pages 54–55: *Aajara* (bedcover), Tétouan, early-nineteenth century, silk satin, polychromatic silk-floss embroidery, length 5 ft. 8 in. (176 cm), width 3 ft. 9 in. (120 cm), private collection.

reversible. Running stitch and feather stitch are used for the border trims. The former is also used elsewhere in the design. Each block of color is outlined in black or dark brown silk, using running stitch or stem stitch, reinforcing the composition and highlighting details. Across the bottom of the *tenchîfa*, a band of drawn-thread work done in natural ivory or white silk, known as a *rivière*, separates the fringe from the border surrounding the veil above. Recent pieces replace the *rivière* with a strip of brocade.

Unlike Fez embroideries, which are executed on a low sewing frame, Tétouan embroiderers tack the area of fabric to be decorated onto a tightly stuffed cushion, which is folded in half and held on the embroiderer's knees. While she works, the rest of the piece is kept carefully rolled inside a piece of protective cotton. Embroidery was designed to be worn and seen, hence its appearance on clothes such as trouser sashes or face veils, and household items such as *tenchîfa*, *izar* curtains, cushions, and mats.

The *tenchîfa*—made-to-measure mirror veils designed to ward off the evil eye during the forty-day honeymoon period—are unique to Tétouan. As Marie-France Vivier explains: "During such highly

Saddle blanket, Turkey, late sixteenth or early-seventeenth century, red silk velvet, Ottoman-style floral decoration in gold lamé, length 6 ft. (183 cm), width 25 in. (63 cm), Cairo Museum of Islamic Arts.

charged rites of passage, the mirror must not be allowed to betray a jealous look. The young bride's fragile sensibilities need to be protected from envy and evil of every sort." With a rich iconography of stylized natural forms, the most closely worked area of the embroidered composition—at the veil's extremities—is crowned with a smaller pyramidal motif, from which spring three forms bearing leaves, fruits and sometimes flowers.

The *tenchîfa* shown on pages 59, 70, and 71 is made of very fine, transparent, undyed linen, that is embroidered at both ends with a large pyramid of multicolored silk flowers. Each panel of embroidery is 2 ft. (62 cm) high. The closely-worked, dense area of embroidery at each end resembles a dazzling floral garden, where the ground (in this case, the natural linen) is scarcely visible. The composition features large ovoid motifs arranged on stems, resembling pomegranates framed by leaves. The border is decorated with red carnations, with jagged petals framing ivory dots and purplish-mauve wild roses. The piece is in perfect condition. Its embroidered decoration is well designed and very characteristic of Tétouan work. In the embroidered area, two colors predominate: a dark, purplish blue and a vivid carmine red, both with slight variations. The secondary elements draw on a palette of red, yellow, old gold, sky blue, purplish mauve, and pale bluish green. The motifs, worked in shimmering, fine natural silks, have been outlined in black. The veil is decorated along the length with compact friezes composed of ovoid motifs and pomegranates. The piece is not reversible and dates from the early-eighteenth century. It is remarkable for its color, finesse and the astonishing perfection of its technique.

The *tenchîfa* pictured on page 51, and shown in detail on pages 66 and 67, is of natural silk, dyed old gold in color, differs in appearance from the above example: the pomegranates have disappeared, to be replaced by flowers from the Ottoman herbary, such as the hyacinth, wild rose, and carnation, blending into annuli of foliage on thick stems. Here, small shrubs alternate with jagged motifs, while two large branches support flowers with serrated petals and spiky, spear-shaped leaves. This central panel is crowned by a large, hatched, conical motif, flanked by obliquely placed wild roses. Bordered by a multicolored sawtooth trim, the bottom strip features an interesting stylized carnation motif in pinkish orange, Nattier blue, ivory, and eggplant. One or two dominant, strong colors have replaced the multitude of bright colors in the earlier example. The traditional *rivière* has disappeared, and is replaced by a strip of white silk braid. (Drawn-thread work is extremely difficult in silk.)

Facing page: *Tenchîfa* (mirror veil), Tétouan, eighteenth century, polychromatic natural silk on linen, satin stitch, running stitch, feather stitch, length 8 ft. 4 in. (257 cm), width 5 ft. (155 cm), private collection.

The *aajara* bedcover pictured on pages 54–55 consists of a large panel of natural silk satin dyed golden yellow, strewn with a repeating pattern of luxuriant, stylized floral bouquets composed of large, jagged-edged flowers—carmine red or royal blue carnations, and wild roses with abundant foliage—less tightly packed than in the *tenchîfa* designs above. The composition is completed by florets and trefoils, entwined with small, highly realistic leafy branches worked in feather stitch using green and white silks. Everything is outlined in black. The relatively wide longitudinal border features a floral frieze of alternating hyacinths and carmine red, white, and blue florets linked by green stems, and large multicolored carnations with white

star-shaped centers surrounding a single black dot. Martha Guérard reminds us: "Rhythmic repetition governs the organization of certain decorative elements; the floral frieze observes an alternating, evenly measured two-step rhythm." The strip is edged in royal blue, and the undecorated areas are dotted with small motifs; starry flowers (hyacinths and wild roses) in red, blue and white connected by thick moss-green stems from which spring trefoil florets and oblong leaves. The piece has a pleasing, bright color scheme and dates from the first half of the nineteenth century.

Stylistically, these magnificent pieces from Tétouan show a number of similarities with certain embroideries from Algiers, as described by Martha

Guérard: "These are drapes, flat-sided hats known as *benikas*, and scarves known as *tenchîfa*, dating for the most part from the eighteenth century. Two distinct families of embroidery are identifiable: those executed in red and blue silk and those in violet. The reds and blues are oldest. The designs are exclusively floral." Georges Marçais notes that the motifs represent "highly stylized palm fronds and flowers, which were perhaps even copied with modifications from some earlier art form, which had already stylized them to the point where they became unrecognizable."

With regard to the support, or base fabric, Algiers work generally uses fine, transparent linen. A few examples are worked in a thick, padded stitch, necessitating a much stronger, cotton base fabric.

While mirror veils, Tétouan's most archetypal embroidered items, clearly show some stylistic similarities to shawls from Algiers, the exact nature of the artistic links between the two cities remains unclear. As Martha Guérard points out, while both regions share a common iconographic repertory, it is treated quite differently in each: "It is impossible to confuse work produced in Algiers and Tétouan, which are both equally admirable, but with distinctive traits." Jeanne Jouin suggests that embroidery prototypes may well have been brought to Tétouan prior to the arrival of Algerian families in the town following the conquest.

Above: *Tenchîfa* (mirror veil, detail), Tétouan, nineteenth century. **Pages 62 and 63:** *Tenchîfa* (mirror veil), Tétouan, late-eighteenth century, polychromatic natural-silk embroidery on natural silk, length 9 ft. 7 in. (296 cm), width 14 in. (36 cm), private collection.

TÉTOUAN

MOROCCAN TEXTILE EMBROIDERY

Pages 64 and 65: *Tenchîfa* (mirror veil, detail), Tétouan, nineteenth century, natural silk embroidery on natural silk, private collection.
Pages 66 and 67: *Tenchîfa* (mirror veil, details), Tétouan, early-nineteenth century, polychromatic natural-silk embroidery
on natural silk, length 14 ft. 5 in. (440 cm), width 24 in. (61 cm), private collection.
Pages 68–69: *Tenchîfa* (mirror veil, detail), Tétouan, nineteenth century, polychromatic silk embroidery
on natural silk, length 6 ft. 6 in. (200 cm), width 3 ft. 3 in. (100 cm), private collection.
Pages 70–71: *Tenchîfa* (mirror veil, detail), Tétouan, eighteenth century, natural-silk embroidery on linen, private collection.

CHECHAOUEN

ANDALUSIAN ECHOES

The representative Chechaouen pieces reproduced here are all household furnishings, in particular an item generally thought to be a chest cover, but whose exact function remains unclear. Its embroidered decoration is similar to that seen on large arid hangings. Originally, the covers were made from thick, strong fabric, usually undyed or bleached linen, but this was gradually abandoned in favor of cotton.

CHECHAOUEN

MOROCCAN TEXTILE EMBROIDERY

The little town of Chechaouen was founded in 1471 by a warrior monk, Moulay Ali ben Rachid, a descendant of the Idrisids and a member of the Akmès tribe who owned the surrounding lands. The town was intended as a stronghold against the Portuguese garrisons at Ceuta and Qsar es-Sghir. As Jeanne Jouin explains about the town that became a refuge for Andalusians: "Despite the absence of texts, all the evidence points to the city's role as refuge for Andalusian exiles: its medieval casbah, so similar to the Moorish fortresses of Muslim Spain; its little houses covered with tiles like those in the village of Testour in Tunisia, built, as we know, by Muslims driven out of the Iberian peninsula; the name given to one of its quarters, Rif-el-Andalous; its inhabitants' still-vivid memory of a distant time when mulberries and silkworms were cultivated within its walls (as they were, to such profit, in Muslim Spain)."

At the foot of the al-Qala'a mountain (*djebel*), these Andalusian exiles clearly sought to recreate their lost world in the Rif. It is to them that Chechaouen owes its growth and prosperity. The town made good use of the skills and technical knowhow of its Andalusian citizens, who were people of great craftsmanship and cultural refinement. Weaving workshops flourished, producing silk and linen, and the city's woodworkers are still renowned today.

At the beginning of the seventeenth century, the town received its final wave of Andalusian immigrants: Spanish Muslims and Jews. The casbah museum has a collection of embroideries featuring stylized flowers set within hexagonal and diamond motifs, comparable to the Andalusian embroideries of Granada, and Hispanic-Moorish carpets dating from the fifteenth and sixteenth centuries.

Prosper Ricard was struck by the similarities between Tétouan and Chechaouen embroideries and the Hispanic-Moorish pieces preserved in France at the Musée Cluny in Paris and the Musée de la Chambre de Commerce in Lyon. P. Ricard was among the first to detect the Andalusian echoes of the Moroccan pieces: "There can be no doubt once one has seen the rich collections of Hispanic-Moorish embroideries in the museums at Barcelona and Madrid. It should come as no surprise to find a thriving Andalusian tradition in Tétouan and Chechaouen, in the fifteenth century." According to Martha Guérard: "At first, Chechaouen embroidery was produced in the Moroccan town of that name. In time, it also began to be produced in Tétouan, apparently imported by Chechaouen women, who married into Tétouan families, and later by the exodus of rural families from Chechaouen to Tétouan, bringing with them their distinctive costumes, their traditional embroideries."

Page 73: *Detail of a chest cover or wall hanging*, Chechaouen, nineteenth century, polychromatic silk embroidery on fine cotton, plaited and chevron stitch, length 6 ft. 2 in. (190 cm), width 29 in. (73 cm), private collection.
Facing page: *Chechaouen Women*, anonymous, c. 1930–50, private collection.

CHECHAOUEN

MOROCCAN TEXTILE EMBROIDERY

The representative Chechaouen pieces reproduced here are all household furnishings, in particular an item generally thought to be a chest cover, but whose exact function remains unclear. Its embroidered decoration is similar to that seen on large *arid* hangings. Originally, the covers were made from thick, strong fabric, usually undyed or bleached linen, but this was gradually abandoned in favor of cotton.

As Jeanne Jouin explains, these pieces are technically similar to tapestry work: "The silk entirely covers the ground; the plain-colored elements are worked in a type of curly Greek stitch, forming small decorative squares, each of which is known as a *beit*, or 'house.'" This is the basic stitch used in all Chechaouen embroidery, worked in a fairly heavy silk, which enables it to be twisted and pulled through the loose weave of the support with an implement rather like a crochet hook, giving the pieces their velvety, looped appearance. In older pieces, monochromatic or two-tone areas were filled exclusively in bouclé stitch; in more recent work, plaited stitch is used.

In her study of the decorative themes of embroidery motifs, Jeanne Jouin argues that: "The looped technique characteristic of certain works in running stitch is generally held to be Coptic in origin; indeed, it can be seen in a piece of Coptic embroidery in the Louvre. Worked in wool, the Egyptian piece uses a simple wool stitch, while the Moroccan pieces use brick sitch; this is the only difference in their technique. In both cases, the twisted thread is not held by a blocking stitch.

Bouclé embroideries were greatly prized by the Copts, who introduced the technique to Islamic peoples. The technique was subsequently practiced in all areas under Arab conquest and persists today in Sicily, Calabria, the Balearic Islands and Andalusia."

The embroidery features a dense, vertically organized design incorporating geometric elements (essentially architectural in character), highly stylized plant and floral elements and a remarkable stylized branching geometric element. On hangings and chest covers, the embroidered decoration is divided into two roughly symmetrical sections connected along their central axis by a band of intermediary elements. The embroidery covers the greater part of the ground.

The hangings served a variety of purposes, often covering the walls behind divans draped in silk brocade. They were also placed over large marriage chests or used to cover the edges of mattresses.

The decorative designs of the large hangings known as *arid* are divided vertically into three distinct zones. Close examination reveals two large rectangles at the ends, containing decorative geometric elements (squares and triangles) and plant motifs (flowers and branching forms). Two intermediary motifs, resembling towers or gateposts, flank a large central motif in the form of a six- or eight-pointed star. *Arid* embroideries also feature additional, star-shaped motifs incorporating gold and silver thread, with small golden sequins on leather backing. These were executed separately by Jewish women. Marie-Rose Rabaté tells us that work in gold of this type was the monopoly of the Jewish population and cites the oldest text reference so far discovered, in the sixteenth-century writings of Leo Africanus: "Jewish goldsmiths ply their trade in the New Town at Fez and take their goods to the Old Town to sell them. Indeed, neither gold nor silver may be worked in the Old Town, and no Mohammedan may work as a goldsmith, since it is said that the sale of gold or silver items for a price beyond the value of their weight is usury. However, the sultans permit the Jews to practice the trade." Martha Guérard adds that "the substitution of these star motifs around the middle of the nineteenth century allows us to trace contemporary evolutions in style and taste."

The basic colors used—deep mustard yellow, dark blue-green, or purplish navy—tend to give the hangings a rather austere aspect, but this is enlivened by the inclusion of geometric mosaic-like areas featuring highly stylized floral and plant motifs. Closely resembling the embroideries of Dagestan (in the Caucasus), they are remarkably decorative, with a central element framed by crosses, rosettes, or stars. Others, cruciform in outline, are scattered across the ground.

The base fabric used for all the pieces illustrated here is thick, strong, undyed linen that has a clearly visible weave.

Blue embroidery

Worked in plaited stitch and bouclé stitch, the piece illustrated on page 86 uses a fairly thick natural silk in an intense blue-green. The embroidery covers a large area of the ground (detail on pages 90 and 91). Vast mosaic-like motifs form the base for the architectural elements, which are worked in plaited stitch, in a range of muted colors, from old rose tinged with violet to pale green, blue, and purplish brown, all outlined in black on a yellow background. Three stars of differing sizes feature rich internal details in delicately nuanced tones on a background of silver thread worked on the linen base fabric. The piece dates from the eighteenth century.

Yellow embroidery

This piece, shown on pages 86 and 87, dates from the early-nineteenth century, features intense mustard-yellow embroidery with dense, highly structured, geometrically stylized floral motifs, forming a bright, multicolored sweep of squares and rectangles similar to mosaics or tapestry. Three stars with leather backing, probably made by Jewish women, are worked in mauve velvet silk decorated with embroidery in round-gold and silver threads.

Page 78: *Chest cover or wall hanging consisting of two bands*, Chechaouen, early-nineteenth century, polychromatic embroidery on linen, length 6 ft. 6 in. (200 cm), width 33 in. (84 cm), private collection.
Page 79: *Chest cover or wall hanging consisting of two bands*, Chechaouen, early-nineteenth century, silk embroidery (mostly brick red) on linen, looped stitch, back stitch, length 7 ft. (212 cm), width 3 ft. 6 in. (110cm), private collection.

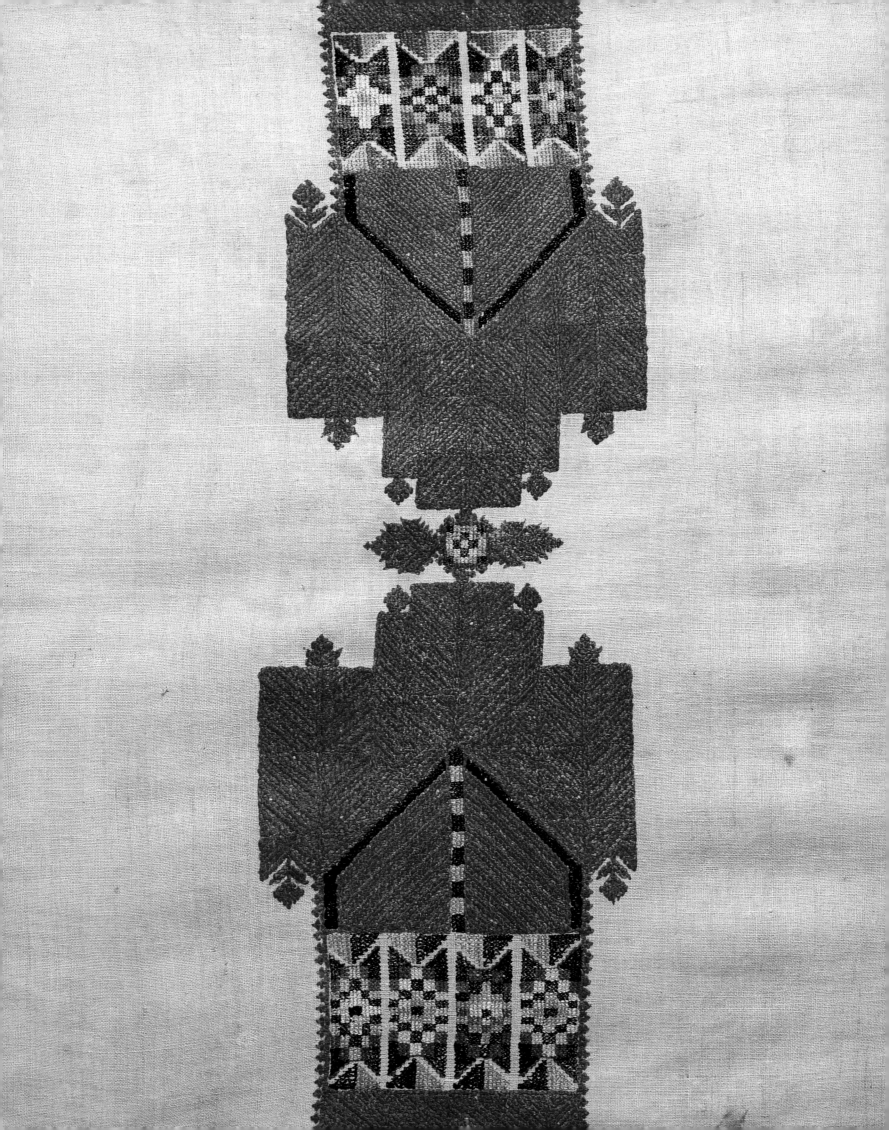

Double embroideries or chest covers

Illustrated on pages 79 and 81, this piece, in dull carmine red and pastel green, is worked in bouclé stitch using heavy, downy natural silks, and features a square central medallion of mosaic-like work with a fine checkerboard pattern of yellow, green, blue, brick red, white, and violet squares, in plaited stitch. In this example, the central area—which is usually without decoration—is filled with a large, roughly diamond-shaped motif framed by a sawtooth line, reversed out of the embroidery by a technique leaving areas of the ground uncovered. This central element features a small, multicolored checkerboard mosaic and is framed by small, highly geometrical, diamond-shaped arborescent motifs. A large, remarkably accomplished drawn-thread *rivière* is divided longitudinally into seven rectangular car-touches, the warp threads of which have been drawn. This highly specialized technique was defined by Prosper Ricard as *point coupé* (broken stitch): "The weft or warp threads are caught in threes, fours, or fives by the same piece of silk, as in a backstitch, forming a bundle. The size and form of the bundles determines the design of the *rivière*." The piece dates from the early-nineteenth century.

"The five medallions"

In a very different style, the remarkable piece shown on page 88 and on the foldout is quite probably the rarest and most valuable example of antique Moroccan embroidery in existence. Only two or three other complete examples are known, perfectly preserved in the Musée des Antiquités in Algiers and the Musée des Arts Décoratifs et des Tissus in Lyon, France. The piece is rectangular in shape. Roughly three-quarters of the ground is decorated with embroidery, featuring a range of highly original, innovative forms. Five large decorative elements are disposed on the ecru-colored linen support: three large octagonal stars and two large cartouches in the form of elongated hexagons. Worked in plaited stitch, these elements contain geometrical motifs based on tracery, arabesques, stars, rectangles, and diamonds. The star occupying the piece's central axis is divided into several sections. As Jeanne Jouin observes: "This is a typical, large eight-pointed star, divided into compartments and featuring combinations of geometrical motifs including the tracery forms much-prized by the Umayyads. Unusually, the points of the star and some of the triangles in the background design culminate in

Facing page: *Detail* (of the chest cover on page 79).
Pages 82–83: *Chest cover or wall hanging,* Chechaouen, nineteenth century, polychromatic silk embroidery on fine cotton muslin, length 6 ft. 2 in. (190 cm), width 29 in. (73 cm), private collection.

small, highly schematized, conical arborescent motifs."

Some compartments are colored carmine pink with pale yellow outlines; other compartments have pink backgrounds decorated with tracery, squares, and small hexagonal elements. The latter are decorated with an undulating line of couched black silk. The three large octagonal stars are laid out in the traditional manner, but they have been modified by local influences. Indeed, the traditional design of geometrical tracery was often replaced by compositions of distinctive geometric figures including clearly recognizable Berber motifs (e.g., zigzags, crosses) as seen in Moroccan weavings and wall hangings. The two other stars—the glories of the piece—are quite differently decorated. Their surface is divided into a multitude of fifty-four smaller elements: squares, octagonal stars, and cruciform motifs, reminiscent of mosaics. The background color is carmine rose, and the star-

shaped, eight-pointed rosettes are edged with couched thread in a golden yellow. Blue, green, and white dots punctuate the design. The large hexagonal cartouches separating the stars are divided into thirty-six diamond shapes framed by narrow friezes in pale pink and filled with stars or crosses in pale yellow, deep blue, or pale green. The two remaining cartouches, triangular in shape, are decorated with lines couched in black thread. A frieze of zigzag lines in pink and yellow separates these from the central cartouche. Sadly, the purpose and exact technique of this extraordinary piece are now unknown.

A piece in the Musée Cluny in Paris, described by Prosper Ricard and Jeanne Jouin, as well as a silk Hispanic-Moorish Nasride lampas in the Victoria and Albert Museum in London (facing page), shed an interesting light on Chechaouen embroidery designs. As Martha Guérard puts it, "This Hispanic-Moorish embroidery indeed seems to present analogies with

Facing page: *Nasride silk lampas with geometric motifs*, southern Spain or North Africa, fourteenth or fifteenth century, length 22 in. (56 cm), width 18 in. (47 cm), Victoria and Albert Museum, London.

Chechaouen embroideries and leads us to conclude tentatively that the two types of embroidery may share a number of common features. Both feature complicated designs of hexagonal cartouches filled with small inscriptional motifs." She goes on to suggest that the cartouches may once have contained inscriptions that have, over time, become highly simplified and stylized.

Page 86 (left) and pages 90 and 91: *Arid* (wall hanging), Chechaouen, early-eighteenth century, polychromatic silk (predominantly blue) on linen, plaited stitch, looped stitch, length 6 ft. 3 in. (192 cm), width 15 in. (39 cm), private collection.
Page 86 (right) and page 87: *Arid* (wall hanging), Chechaouen, late-eighteenth century, silk embroidery (predominantly yellow and gold) on linen, plaited and looped stitch, gold thread, length 6 ft. 3 in. (192 cm), width 15 in. (39 cm), private collection.

Page 88: *Arid* (wall hanging), Chechaouen, early-seventeenth century, polychromatic silk embroidery on linen, plaited and looped stitch, length 9 ft. (275 cm), width 32 in. (81 cm), Musée des Tissus, Lyon.
Foldout and page 89: *Arid* (wall hanging), Chechaouen, early-seventeenth century, polychromatic silk embroidery on linen, plaited and looped stitch, length 8 ft. 5 in. (260 cm), width 28 in. (70 cm), private collection.

MONOCHROMATIC SUBTLETIES

Eugène Aubin provides a description of a Fez interior: "The bedroom walls are covered with fabric appliquéd with embroidery, or cut-out designs. The floor is strewn with mattresses and carpets, cushions made of Lyon silk, and embroideries in the distinctive Fez style, worked in silk thread on white canvas."

MOROCCAN TEXTILE EMBROIDERY

ez embroidery—monochromatic, one-sided, like most of its neighbors, and based on counted threads—represents one of the most distinctive of Morocco's wealth of regional styles. From modest origins as a mainly Berber community, founded in 809 C.E., the city was transformed in the ninth and tenth centuries by the arrival of some eight thousand families fleeing Al-Andalus and two thousand Arab families from Kairouan (Tunisia). These new populations brought with them their distinctive religious, cultural, and architectural heritage, the basis for the city's future greatness.

Over twelve centuries, Fez was ruled by seven successive dynasties; its golden age, however, came with accession of the Marinids in the thirteenth century, who made the city their political capital. During this period of political stability, Fez enjoyed a thriving cultural life and an unprecedented boom in trade. The city's caravansaries served as staging posts for entire caravans on their way to Al-Andalus. Supported by Andalusian refugees fleeing the Christian Reconquista, the powerful Marinids attracted scholars, craftsmen, and merchants to the city, whose expertise did much to further the new capital's economic growth. Andalusian techniques in mosaic (*zellige*), wood, and plaster were kept alive

by craftsmen from Seville, Toledo, and Granada, organized into guilds, or *tanta*, within their respective quarters, caravansaries, or workshops, under the authority of the *muhtasib*. In Morocco, Jewish and Muslim populations fleeing Spain were able to coexist in peace, and still do. Fez is no exception to this tradition of hospitality and tolerance; the city is known as the center of the largest Jewish community in the Maghreb. Fezzi Jews have played a fundamental role in the city's economic life, particularly in the textile and jewelry sectors.

Today, the Batha museum in the ancient Hispanic-Moorish palace houses a small collection of Fez embroideries and many other superb examples of Moroccan craftsmanship.

In 1912, Eugène Aubin described the city's social and family life as follows: "The monotonous, refined lives of the Moors of Fez are centered on their homes and gardens, where the people quietly live out the days—melancholy or gay—that Allah has seen fit to grant them. Families are large, and, in the evening, everyone gathers to take tea and a light collation—the only moment in the day when the entire family is together. The women remain at home alone and receive little education. Only a few are able to read and write. Housework and household affairs are

Page 93: *Gelsa* (tablecloth, detail), Fez, late-seventeenth century, silk embroidery on linen, running stitch, Fez stitch (*terz al ghorza*), length 4 ft. 5 in. (137 cm), width 4 ft. (125 cm), private collection.
Facing page: *Woman Dressed in a Ceremonial Kaftan in Fez*, c. 1934–1939, photograph by Jean Besancenot (1902–1992), Institut du Monde Arabe, Paris.

their main preoccupation, although the wealthier ladies employ servants. Embroidery, music, and cards provide languid diversions, and long hours are spent beneath the loggia or terrace, which is their special preserve. Here, they will chat with neighbors and receive the day's news. They go out little and receive few visitors, particularly the upper classes. Family celebrations, weddings, births, baptisms, and circumcisions are welcome distractions, enlivened by singers and the gathering of family and female friends. The Jewish and Muslim women, who visit these homes selling jewelry and toilet articles find willing customers—Moorish ladies are highly charming and enjoy such fineries. The women's social life is entirely dependent on family celebrations; parties are almost never organized without such pretexts among groups of women friends. A high-ranking woman will almost never be seen in the street. Indeed, women of the lower classes seem to enjoy greater freedom to shop and pay visits and will go out on foot. An upper-class woman will ride to a friend's house astride a mule."

Fez is an ancient city with an equally long tradition of embroideries. Jeanne Jouin notes that familiar embroidery motifs, such as the eight-pointed star, are also found on the monuments of ancient Syria, and that the fleur-de-lys has been a feature of Mediterranean art since antiquity. The Egyptian collections at the Louvre include a textile from an Egyptian Coptic necropolis featuring an early example of the typical Fezzi border pattern of foliated chevrons. Embroidered *telmitas* (mattress ends) from Fez also feature geometric motifs very similar to those seen in some Byzantine textiles.

In certain Fez pieces, Jeanne Jouin sees an echo of the vase representations on Coptic tunics. In the absence of any formal, written accounts, popular Spanish embroidery would appear to exhibit traces of the artistic traditions revealed in sixteenth-century collections of French, English, Italian, and German embroidery patterns. Traditional gilets worn in rural Spain clearly recall the arborescent plant designs of Fez work. The Museu Tèxtil id'Indumentària (Museum of Textiles and Fashion) in Barcelona houses some fragments of antique, geometric, monochromatic embroidery in red or blue on a white ground, clearly similar to the abstract designs on Fez embroideries. This should come as no surprise, given that Spain's original Muslim conquerors—the Almoravids—were of Syrian origin, and the great Andalusian port of Almería, famous for its textile workshops, established strong trade links with the port city of Alexandria. In the Middle Ages, fashions inspired by the styles and motifs of Syrian and Egyptian art spread from Italy—the dominant artistic and commercial power in the medieval Mediterranean world—to the rest of Europe.

The history of Fez shows us, then, that identical ornamental motifs developed and spread simultaneously in Morocco and Spain. Prosper Ricard suggests an interesting explanation: "The likely hypothesis seems to be that Fez stitch was introduced by Turkish or Circassian women, who were brought to the harems of wealthy Fezis in great numbers. The stitch is still commonly used in the Balkans and Asia Minor. As we have seen, it is referred to in women's pattern books as the 'double-sided triangular Turkish stitch.' Another factor supporting this hypothesis is the use of sewing frames. These are common to all of the Maghrebi cities formerly under Turkish control (Algiers, Tunis, Cairo, etc.), but in Morocco they are exclusive to Fez, and nowhere else."

Formerly, Fez embroideries fell into two types: counted-thread work requiring no underdrawing, still practiced there through the 1970s, and work necessitating the use of underdrawing, which died out in the middle of the nineteenth century.

The most common type of Fez embroidery is known as *terz del ghorza* (point stitch), based on a vertical, horizontal, and diagonal running stitch, used either simply or twisted to form star-shaped or radiating stitches. Piqué and stem stitch are used to highlight or outline the edges of shapes; more rarely, satin stitch is used in a sawtooth pattern to decorate narrow strips. The work is done on a low sewing frame, without underdrawing, on often very fine ivory or bleached cotton or linen. Counted-thread work demands the use of a single color, preferably in very fine natural silk. Older pieces are characterized by the use of refined pale or deep colors. One dense, tightly worked stitch is used throughout an individual piece of work, taking in the same number of warp or weft threads. The embroidery also has no reverse; it is not double-sided, although one side always has a higher relief.

Fez embroidery is used to decorate all types of household furnishings: mattress covers, tablecloths, place mats, cushions, curtains, and certain items of traditional women's clothing such as shawls, trouser sashes, scarves and handkerchiefs.

Eugène Aubin provides a description of a Fez interior: "The bedroom walls are covered with fabric appliquéd with embroidery, or cut-out designs. The floor is strewn with mattresses and carpets, cushions made of Lyon silk, and embroideries in the distinctive Fez style, worked in silk thread on white canvas." Mattress trimmings were an important part of the accoutrements of an elegant reception room. Known as a *tlamt diel trib* or *telmita*, the trimming served to hide the edges of the upper mattress on divans and beds. Sumptuously embroidered, the preserve of wealthy families, each strip is about 9 ft. 8 in. (300 cm) long and 30 in. (75 cm) wide. Their production demanded a great deal of patience and skill on the part of the embroiderer, and girls would take months or even years to complete them, working at home for their own trousseaux, or simply for pleasure. No two *telmitas* are alike—each woman produces her own variations on the basic geometric and floral designs, but the underlying structure is always the same: the panel is covered with a mesh of diamond shapes formed of intersecting lines, each

featuring minuscule, symmetrically arranged elements such as leaves or florets. The resulting compartments contain isolated floral and plant motifs in a great variety of stylized forms.

Telmitas feature two types of embroidered composition. In the first, the ground is less densely covered; the central floral motif tends not to dominate, and the mesh consists of simple lines, decorated only sparsely with florets. In the second type, the diamond trellis is much denser and richer, while the visible ground is reduced in favor of a larger, more complex central floral motif. Embroiderers draw on a great variety of different floral motifs, so each piece is unique.

One complete example of the second type of composition, shown on page 105, consists of a fine ivory cotton base fabric, embroidered with a particularly interesting design in petrol-blue and olive-green silk on a gray ground, using a variety of stitches (but not a star stitch) based on three counted threads. The mesh area, delimited by three lines of florets, is decorated with a vast rectangle at the junction points. The sides have cut-off corners and are decorated with a large bouquet of stylized triangular flowers around a central, diamond-shaped flower. This piece

dates from the late-eighteenth or early-nineteenth century.

The *mendil* (tablecloth) was much prized in Fez and was a vital part of everyday city life, with multiple uses. With opposing corners knotted together, it formed an elegant parcel for the protection of precious items or for a young girl's trousseau. When opened and spread out, it provided an attractive setting for the display of a fiancé's gifts. It was also used to carry a change of clothing to the hammam and to swaddle young babies during their first outings. Placed over the bride's knees during the ceremonial application of henna, it allowed the *naqqacha* (the woman decorating the bride's hands and feet) to work without fear of stains and spills. The *mendil* also covered everyday objects such as trays, glasses, bottles, including jars of sugar, mint, or tea, and kept the dust off bread and pastries.

The following pieces are fragments dating from the eighteenth and nineteenth centuries, showing a great variety of decorative motifs—flowers, geometrical forms, and, sometimes, animals and birds. Of particular interest are the friezes decorating each end of the cloth, which are also found on tablecloths, place mats, and cushions. These consist of a small embroidered frieze incorporating

Facing page: *Salon of the Dar Jebina Jelloul*, Fez, c. 1930, anonymous, private collection.
Page 100: *Tlamt del khrib* or *telmita* (mattress cover, detail), Fez, late-eighteenth century, running stitch, length 6 ft. 9 in. (210 cm), width 33 in. (85 cm), private collection.

minuscule floral and arborescent geometric motifs, as well as two thin borders comprising floral and geometric elements, which appear on either side of a central band containing similar motifs. The whole composition is sometimes finished with another, larger decorative frieze.

Martha Guérard is surprised to find silhouettes of birds resembling storks, seen in profile, with long beaks: "We know that these likable birds were much loved in Morocco, where they enjoyed almost sacred status, nesting freely on old city ramparts or in the tops of trees." A. Goldenburg notes that, after jewelry, embroidery is the Moroccan decorative art that features the most figurative representations.

The oldest example of this style would seem to be a small eighteenth-century fragment, illustrated on pages 116–117, whose composition, complete and intact, is particularly delicate and finely balanced. The design is worked in bronze silk on an ivory cotton base fabric, in piqué and various types of running stitch, but mostly a double twisting stitch. The composition features a border with alternating eight-branched stars and stylized diamond shapes; fine strips frame the central band, which is decorated with a thick, sawtoothed stem and plant shapes that emerge between the "teeth." The delicate final frieze has a lacy appearance, with alternating types of tree—one with a thin trunk and leaves at the top, the other with a thicker, fringed silhouette, topped with a long-beaked bird perched on a nest (top of page 118).

Aleuj embroideries

The origins of this type of embroidery and the name given to it by Moroccan women remain a mystery. The world *aleuj* means a convert to Islam, and the term may refer to Christian slaves captured in Spain, who sub-sequently converted. However, as Jeanne Jouin notes: "The stitch known as *aleuj* is unknown in Spain. It belongs to the Persian family of stitches and is used today [the first half of the twentieth century] in the Balkan province of Janina. These Balkan embroideries feature large, full-blown flowers, such as those seen in the center of the geometric schemes of certain Moroc-can examples. As with the Fez stitch, it seems to have been introduced by Levantine women in the harems of Fez. This would also explain some of the floral motifs and technical aspects of *aleuj* embroideries."

We still know very little about *aleuj* embroidery, not least the origins of its atypical technique, although some have identified it as Circassian. We are also unaware of the exact date of its introduction into Morocco. Prosper Ricard notes that its use had died out in Morocco by the early-nineteenth century. Martha Guérard observes: "Unlike the airy, delicate compositions and refined technique of Fez's *terz del ghorza* or counted-thread embroideries, *aleuj* work is characterized by strange, dense, massive elements."

Aleuj work is nonreversible. Most pieces are monochromatic, but rare polychromatic examples exist. The embroiderer uses underdrawing, and forms

Above (top): *Fragment of mhadda* (cushion), Fez, eighteenth century, *aleuj* embroidery in natural silk (predominantly dark brown), motifs filled with traditional chevron/satin stitch, length 20 in. (50 cm), width 4 ½ in. (12 cm), private collection.
Above (bottom): *Fragment of mhadda* (cushion), Fez, early-nineteenth century, *aleuj* embroidery in natural silk on linen, length 16 in. (41 cm), width 5 in. (13 cm), collection of Mr. and Mrs. Niblack, Indianapolis Museum of Art.

are filled with a type of slanting satin stitch. Stem stitch or back stitch is used to outline decorative elements, and a fine herringbone stitch outlines the different registers of the composition. The color palette features dull carmine, old rosewood, yellowish bronze, and royal and navy blues combined with iridescent, delicate silvery mauves.

Aleuj embroideries fall into two distinct decorative groups. The first, and larger, group consists of powerful geometric designs featuring prominent, broad linear elements together with triangles, rectangles, and diamonds. The second, rarer, group features charming, delicate floral designs incorporating four-petaled flowers, carnations with serrated petals and scrolling, and

sawtoothed foliage of the type already seen in Tétouan embroideries.

The cushion end (two identical bands, illustrated on page 102), is finely embroidered in a predominantly geometric design. The support is ivory cotton, worked in a strong, golden-brown silk. The central band remains severely geometrical with long oblique rectangles decorated with a sawtooth border featuring motifs reversed out of the embroidered area. The end frieze consists of large, star-shaped flowers with a central element com-posed of four leaves within a reversed-out heart, jagged leaves and plant elements terminating in a trefoil floret. With a magnifying glass, we can see tiny cruciform motifs within the diamond forms. This piece dates from the eighteenth century.

Facing page: *Tlamt del khrib* (mattress cover), Fez, eighteenth century, natural silk on linen, running stitch, length 5 ft. 6 in. (170 cm), width 31 ½ in. (80 cm), private collection.
Above: *Tlamt del khrib* (mattress cover), Fez, eighteenth century, natural silk on linen, running stitch, length 7 ft. 9 in. (240 cm), width 16 ½ in. (42 cm), private collection.

Facing page: *Detail of wall hanging,* Fez, late-eighteenth century, dense monochromatic midnight-blue embroidery on ivory cotton, four panels, length 16 ft. (500 cm), width 3 ft. 3 in. (100 cm) each, private collection.

Above: *Gelsa* (tablecloth), Fez, late-eighteenth century, monochromatic natural silk embroidery on cotton, running stitch, length 4 ft. 5 in. (137 cm), width 4 ft. (125 cm), private collection.

Pages 110–111: *Shan* (shawl), Fez, late-eighteenth century, monochromatic natural silk embroidery (dark blue) on cotton gauze, length 6 ft. 9 in. (209 cm), width 34 in. (86 cm), private collection.

Above and facing page: *Tekka* (trouser sash), Fez, eighteenth century, monochromatic silk embroidery on ivory cotton muslin, length 6 ft. 2 in. (190 cm), width 12 in. (31 cm), private collection.
Page 114–115: *Edge of a shan* (shawl), Fez, late-eighteenth century, monochromatic silk embroidery on cotton muslin, length 19 in. (49 cm), width 17 in. (43 cm), private collection.

Edge of a mendil (tablecloth), Fez, eighteenth century, monochromatic silk embroidery on cotton, length 21 in. (53 cm), width 20 in. (50 cm), private collection.

Pages 118–119: *Collection of Fez stitch fragments (*terz del ghorza*), various running stitches (monochromatic and polychromatic), seventeenth to nineteenth century, private collection.

Pages 120–125: *Collection of shans* (shawls). Late-eighteenth (or early-nineteenth) century pieces
are worked in a smooth Rabat stitch similar to Fez stitch, private collection.

MEKNÈS

POINTILLIST FANTASY

Meknès embroidery is worked on an extremely fine fabric base made of cream-colored muslin, often woven with a pattern of stripes, spots, or little colored squares.

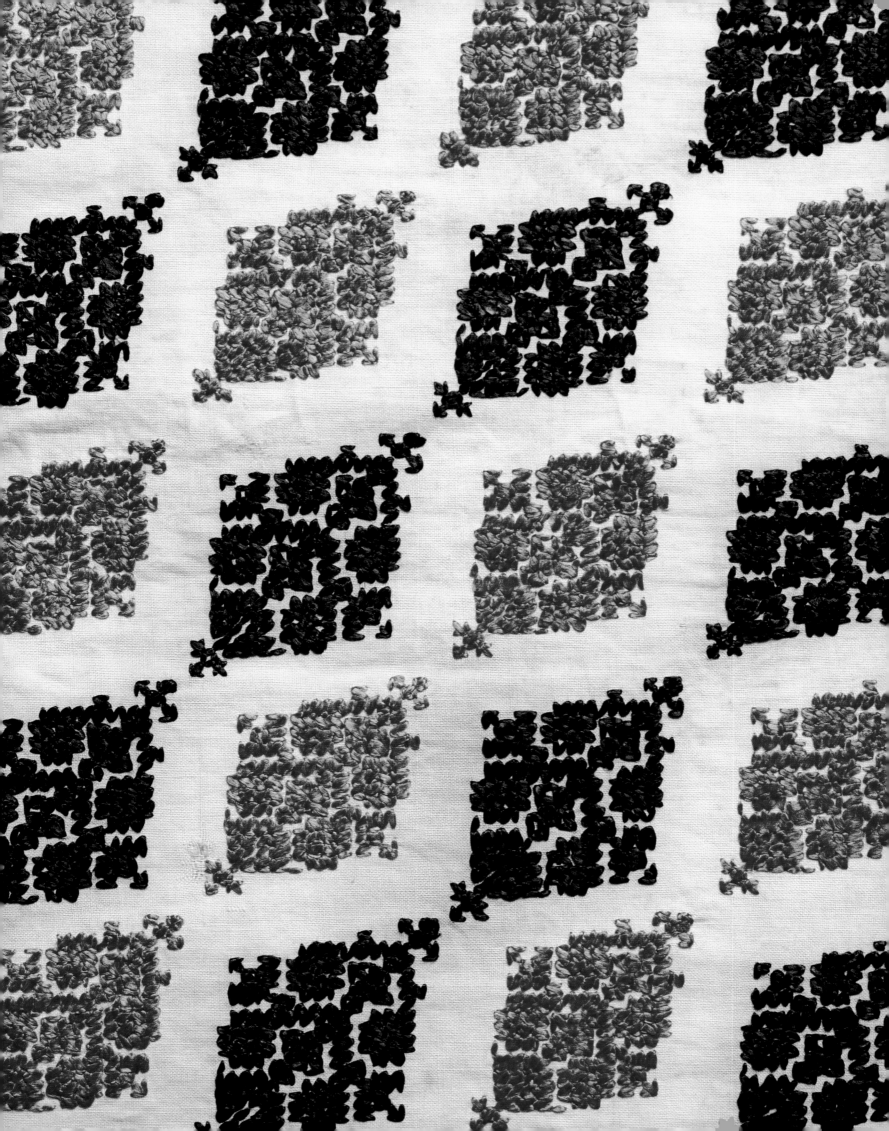

MEKNÈS

MOROCCAN TEXTILE EMBROIDERY

eknès is over a thousand years old. The Berber tribe known as the Meknassis, hence the city's name, first settled in the region in the tenth century, and the city's oldest surviving monuments date back to the empires of the Almohads and Marinids. In the mid-fourteenth century, a number of Andalusian families, mostly from Córdoba and Seville, settled in Meknès and the surrounding region. They plied their trade within the city, organized markets, and influenced the local craft industry, particularly mosaics (*zellige*) and woodworking. Surrounded by orchards, quince, pomegranates, apples, figs, grapes, and olives, Meknès owes its prosperity to these Andalusian refugees. It is said that Sultan Moulay Ismail, who reigned at Meknès and was a contemporary of Louis XIV, sought the hand of the Sun King's daughter Mademoiselle de Blois, born of his liaison with Louise de La Vallière. The request caused considerable consternation at court, since the sultan was well into his sixties at the time. Meknès's spectacularly rich artistic and cultural heritage is preserved today in the remarkable collections of the Jamai Museum, which include fine examples of ironwork, weaving, leatherwork, embroidery, sheet metalwork, and gold plate.

Meknès embroidery is technically and iconographically similar to that of Salé and Fez. Jeanne Jouin identifies Meknès work as a blend of these two traditions, with Berber styles: "Meknès's golden age came in the last third of the seventeenth century, when Sultan Moulay Ismail made it an imperial city and the site of his principal residence. A great variety of people then came to settle in the town—administrators and craftsmen recruited in the major Moroccan cities, rural [hence Berber] laborers brought in to work on the Sultan's colossal construction projects. It is not, then, difficult to see how the city's own embroidery style developed as a fusion of the styles of Salé and Fez, its nearest neighbors, with the distinctive aesthetic and warm colors of local Berber styles adding a pleasingly original touch."

In Meknès, *terz meknassi* (nonreversible, counted-thread work) is produced in a vast range of colors: red, yellow, orange, green, brown, black, and, more rarely, blue. Marie-France Vivier notes that the distinctive, small touches of bright color (red, yellow, violet, greens, and blues) set like precious stones into blocks of lighter or darker color, recall the city's sumptuous ceramic mosaics.

Although similar in appearance to counted-thread motifs, Meknès embroidery is worked on an extremely fine base fabric made of cream-colored muslin, often woven with a pattern of stripes, spots, or little colored squares. Genuine counted-thread work is impossible on fine-grade fabric such as this,

---

Page 127: *Mendil* (tablecloth), Meknès, late eighteenth century, diamond motifs in polychrome silk embroidery on ivory cotton, various running stitches, length 6 ft. 9 in. (210 cm), width 24 in. (60 cm), private collection.
Facing page: *Woman at Home in Meknès*, 1930, photograph by Jean Besancenot (1902–1992), Institut du Monde Arabe, Paris.

although the woven design can act as a guide. Embroiderers, therefore, have to rely on the accuracy of their own eyes and aesthetic judgment. As Jeanne Jouin observes: "Fez stitch is most often used, but in a bastardized form. *Meknasiyat* embroiderers do not count threads scrupulously, as the technique demands." To strengthen the work, thicker silk is used, and a rich color palette compensates for the resulting loss of regularity and finesse. Colored outlines around the motifs—frequently dark carmine red—favor the emergence of a dominant color palette in individual works. Over time, the preferred outline color has evolved from carmine red to brown and black, or two-tone (red and black, dark garnet and orange, or, more rarely, garnet and green). In this case, the alternating outline colors correspond to the pattern of alternating motifs.

Meknès embroiderers work with great freedom and creativity, using a wide range of colors, although this sometimes upsets the balance of forms and the rhythm of the patterns used. Color variations are applied indiscriminately within each strip of decoration, or from one strip to the next. Typically, the field is embroidered with isolated dots or small lozenges, which sometimes interfere with the woven design of the base fabric. The embroidery is worked in double-sided running stitch and darning stitch, and a unique combination of brick stitch and oblique stitch. Sometimes, dyed silk tassels are added to the edges of a piece. A. R. de Lens remembers the richly colored Meknès embroideries used along the bottom of fine muslin curtains hung in the openings of the women's loggia or terrace to filter the light, keep out the heat and protect the ladies from the inquisitive glances of a guest crossing the courtyard.

The *shan* bathing shawl (pages 136 and 137) is embroidered in poly-chrome silks on an ivory cotton support. The designs are outlined in royal-blue thread on one side and lengthwise in carmine red on the other. The trimming at the outer ends of these shawls consist of geometric and arborescent motifs in a variety of colors. There is no central motif; rather, the piece is evenly covered with the same cruciform motif throughout. The latter are in three alternating colors—yellow, blue, and red. This piece dates from the early nineteenth century.

A second *shan* shawl, (pages 132 and 133), has a design featuring dots in four main colors—black, red, orange, and pink. The support is a very fine pinkish-beige cotton gauze. The polychromatic natural silks are worked in running stitch and stem stitch, giving a rich, opulent appearance. The polychromatic strips, bands, and borders comprise geometric and branching motifs. The scattered dots are characteristic of Meknès work. This piece dates from the end of the nineteenth century.

Pages 131, 132 and 133: *Shan* (shawl), Meknès, late eighteenth century, polychromatic natural silk embroidery on very fine sand-colored cotton muslin, running stitch and stem stitch, length 8 ft. 7 in. (265 cm), width 30 in. (77 cm), private collection.

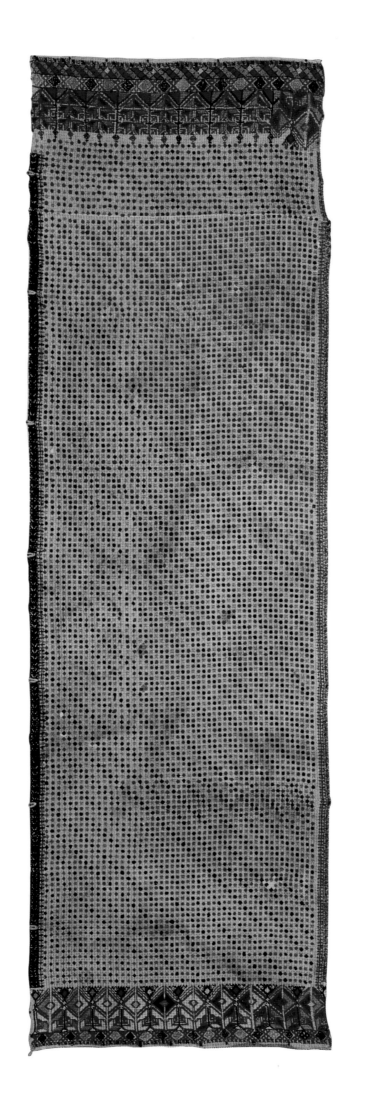

Above: *A detail of the mendil* (tablecloth) shown on page 127.
Facing page: *Large mendil* (tablecloth), Meknès, late eighteenth century, polychromatic silk embroidery on cotton, counted thread work, running stitch, length 4 ft. 2 in. (127 cm), width 3 ft. 3 in. (101 cm), collection of Mr. and Mrs. Niblack, Indianapolis Museum of Art.

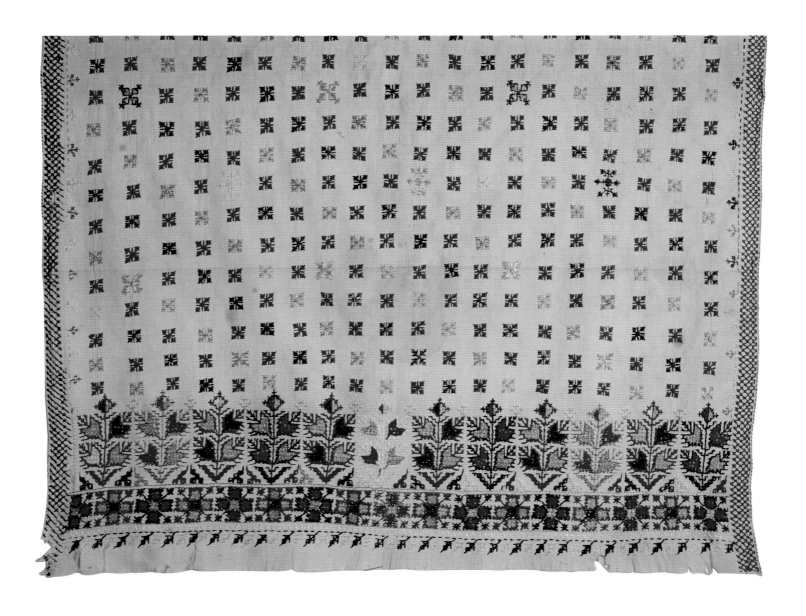

Above and facing page: *Shan* (shawl), Meknès, early-nineteenth century, polychromatic natural-silk embroidery on cotton, double-sided line stitch (counted threads), length 8 ft. 2 in. (250 cm), width 29 ½ in. (75 cm), private collection.

A PASSION FOR FLOWERS

The introduction of imported tulles and muslins decorated with floral motifs seems to have engendered the designs featuring full-blown flowers entirely filled with embroidery, whose subsequent stylization was to have such an impact on contemporary styles.

Morocco's capital has had a remarkable history. An imperial capital in times of wealth, it was reduced in periods of recession to little more than a village. In the twelfth century, under Yaqub al-Mansur, "the Victorious," Rabat enjoyed a brief moment of glory. Al-Mansur erected several miles of fortified walls and built the gateway leading into the casbah. He began construction work on the biggest mosque in the western Islamic world, of which only the impressive Hassan minaret remains. The city's decline set in shortly afterward, but its fortunes were revived in the seventeenth century with the arrival of Muslim refugees from Spain, as Jean-Pierre Bernes recounts: "Sultan Mulay Zaydan encouraged the notoriously brave, warlike people of Hornachos in the Spanish province of Badajos to settle in the casbah at Rabat, hoping to gain their allegiance. However, the Hornacheros quickly declared themselves independent, rallied the Hispanic-Moorish refugees in other parts of the Maghreb to their cause and established the latter outside the citadel, at the foot of its walls. Rabat was, thus, repopulated; the city's embroiderers owe their technique and decorative inspiration to that of their Moorish ancestors."

At the same time, Christian renegades, pirates, corsairs, and filibusters of various nationalities swelled the ranks of Rabat's population. The first Alid sultans tried to stifle piracy, but no one succeeded in putting an end to the activities of the corsairs, who continued to plunder vessels until the nineteenth century. During the first half of the seventeenth century, overflowing with gold, slaves, and other riches, the twin cities of Rabat and Salé established the independent Bou Regreg republic, named after the river that flows between them.

Rabat's links with Andalusian culture were twofold. On the one hand, the Arab Berber culture was transmitted to Spain under the Almoravid, Almohad, and Marinid dynasties. On the other hand, when Muslim and Jewish populations from Al-Andalus migrated to North Africa, they brought with them their weaponry, belongings, customs, and skills. After the Christian conquest of Al-Andalus, the Bou Regreg estuary became a port attached to a relatively unpopulated town centered on the casbah, capable of assimilating a fair number of refugees.

Rabat and Salé's links with Muslim Spain are perfectly reflected in its traditions, habits, and customs and in its architecture. Its weddings, funerals, costumes, music, songs, and lullabies are all redolent of Al-Andalus. The Rabat Museum of Moroccan Arts in the casbah is housed in Mulay Ismail's princely seventeenth-century pavilion. One room recreates a traditional Moroccan interior, its walls covered with gold brocade and silks from Fez.

It would seem logical to suppose that Rabat embroidery was brought to the city's Andalusian quarter by Moorish refugees from Spain. The large-scale embroideries of Tétouan, another city populated by refugees from Spain, would seem to confirm the hypothesis. As Jeanne Jouin observes: "Moroccan embroideries of all kinds exist only in cities settled by the Moors of Spain. For the embroiderers of Rabat, the decorated festoons beneath their squat florets are the legacy of their Moorish grandmothers; the same motifs are seen in Spain. The same is true of the plaited-stitch embroideries, similar to those of Salé, the use of Renaissance-style foliate patterns, embroideries on net, and bobbin lace, all now sadly forgotten."

Until the mid-nineteenth century, embroidery in Spain was executed on a cushion, just as in Rabat. Indeed, the Spanish word *berdada* refers precisely to old Rabat embroidery. The word *sertal*, meaning the act of threading a needle, is the same as the Spanish verb—all evidence of the close links between the two regions. As Henri Terrasse notes: "Madame Brunot David's admirable work has done much to trace and uncover the broad lines of the history of Rabat embroidery. She has rightly observed that, in common with almost all other urban embroideries in Morocco, it is Spanish in origin and belongs to the final layer of Hispanic influence in Moroccan art, that imported in the early-seventeenth century by the Moors expelled from Spain. Spanish-Renaissance influence was nowhere so all-encompassing and long-lasting as in Rabat. Embroidery is the feminine complement to the last great act of civilization [i.e., the Reconquista] before our arrival in the life of the little Atlantic port."

But the embroideries introduced to Morocco were also heavily influenced by their new environment. The Spanish Moors who disembarked at Rabat did not mix with the local population. Even today, the so-called Andaluz population constitutes a more or less separate society, a kind of "acknowledged aristocracy that keeps to its own quarter," as Brunot-David observes. Isolated from the locals, these people were equally cut off from their re-Christianized Spanish origins. This situation clearly affected the subsequent, slow evolution of the embroideries. Newly arrived refugees came into contact with neighboring tribespeople, who provided them with goods of all kinds. Little by little, the latter became urbanized, working in the service of the Andaluz population. Local tribeswomen became household servants, children's nannies, wet-nurses, even concubines or sometimes wives. As such, they played an active role in household activities, including embroidery. Christiane Brunot-David elucidates: "Girls initiated into the art of embroidery for the first time could know nothing of the artistic origins of the works they produced, and their teachers, more and more distanced from the sources of their work [in Spain], gradually forgot the original meanings of their motifs and designs. In this way, each became receptive to new techniques. The deep-seated African instinct for extreme geometric stylization was increasingly freed from the constraints of traditional forms, so that decorative themes became purely abstract, with an inner life of their own, absorbing other influences and evolving totally new, equally abstract elements."

Imports of luxurious European fabrics strongly influenced Rabat embroideries, with the city's embroiderers adopting elements which they combined with their own traditional motifs. Quite unaware, Morocco encountered the West via European brocades, which were themselves imitations of textiles from Damascus (damask). The introduction of imported tulles and muslins decorated with floral motifs seems to have engendered the designs featuring full-blown flowers entirely filled with embroidery, whose subsequent stylization was to have such an impact on contemporary styles.

The original, "Spanish" embroidery styles featuring massive, powerful architectural forms evolved slowly but surely under local influence. A new technique emerged, Oriental in inspiration, bringing with it multicolored, rich, stylized floral motifs. Initially used to fill the massive forms of the designs, it quickly gained currency to the point of driving out the original motifs and stitches. Rabat embroideries were also enriched by the assimilation —with considerable taste and discernment—of new styles from Europe. Rabat embroideries evolved, then, from an architectural to a floral style, while their original, underlying structure and codes remained intact.

Rabat embroideries fall into two types, different in technique, color, and design but similar to the extent that both are worked on base fabrics of cotton, and white or ecru muslin. The first is resolutely monochromatic and is worked in robust, powerful colors, while the second features profuse, dense, flamboyant, multicolored designs based on strong contrasts. Both old and new Rabat embroideries are worked on supports of linen, cotton, muslin, and brilliant silk but are characterized by different stitches, motifs and designs. Old Rabat embroideries feature a particularly striking and mysterious motif, suggestive of a human silhouette. Madame Jouin traces its genesis to the floret motifs of old Rabat work: "[The figures] are, in fact, the culmination of a progressive process of straightening and geometric stylization, applied to sinuous, scrolling vegetal motifs." Embroidery was an honorable occupation in Rabat society, and a great variety of items were produced here until the first third of the twentieth century. As in other Moroccan cities, these were not purely decorative but were destined for use in the everyday life of the household or for display at family celebrations.

These obscure, apparently anthropomorphic, motifs were indeed gradually modified by local stylistic influences and by the embroiderers' imaginations. In common use from the eighteenth to the mid-nineteenth centuries, they inspired a number of fascinating variations before being completely abandoned in favor of plant motifs. (This is true of the motifs on embroidered clothing and household items alike.) Their transformation is illustrated by the three pieces reproduced here on page 147. Their demise heralds the arrival of what have since become known as new Rabat embroideries, characterized by the progressive covering, from the late-eighteenth century onward, of the originally undecorated central field. In older work, a few discreet geometric motifs are placed horizontally, above the embroidered area. In later pieces, the discreet geometric forms that originally filled the embroidered area begin to fill out and take on the appearance of highly stylized vegetation.

The more common monochromatic pieces are found in strong reds, dark blues, and yellows. In later years Rabat embroidery vacillated between duller monochromatics and dazzling polychromatic designs. Numerous pieces draw on an increasingly rich palette of alternating colors, with a marked preference for carmine red and dark blue or, more rarely, old gold. The most common base fabric is fine or heavier-grade ivory or bleached cotton with a sheen and sometimes with a damask weave. Monochromatic patches of color are sometimes embroidered with a variety of motifs—grid patterns and stripes—giving an impression of relief. Old Rabat embroideries are worked in single linen, silk or cotton thread. Another, doubled thread can sometimes be added on coarser supports, with thick, downy natural silks often being used for the embroidering.

Old Rabat embroidery was worked without the use of pencil underdrawing. Satin stitch is the basic filling stitch used. A broad plaited stitch used to outline the motifs fell from use in the second half of the nineteenth century, around the same time as the anthropomorphic silhouettes and their variations. As the afore-mentioned plant motifs took over, feather stitch and running stitch or back stitch became increasingly common. The new style was better suited to the decoration of large items, such as door curtains.

Plant motifs, initially a discreet feature used at the ends of decorative borders, were gradually scattered across the central field. The designs featured full-blown, many-petaled flowers as well as stylized trefoil florets, and flowers, leaves or petals in outline. Geometric forms such as diamonds, triangles, and circles were incorporated into stems or branches. In the borders, these are organized into bands, chevron patterns, diamonds, simple stripes, and bouquets. The central vertical axis of *izar* curtains are marked by tall monumental forms resembling the outlines of towers or minarets. (One is reminded of Rabat's Hassan minaret, all that remains of the unfinished Hassan mosque.)

The three fragments of cushion ends reproduced on page 147 illustrate the slow mutation of forms to a state of pure abstraction—a marvelous testimony to the power of Moroccan creative genius.

Facing page (top): *Council of the Viziers of Sultan Moulay Youssef in the Sultan's Palace at Rabat,* 1921, Roger Viollet.
Facing page (bottom): *Detail of the izar* (door hanging) on page 139.

The first fragment, shown here on the facing page, is a monochromatic cushion with nonreversible decoration. The design does not use counted threads and is worked in dark carmine red on ivory cotton fabric. The motif is not upright but slopes to the left. Small, serrated "heads" may be seen arranged in the center of the cushion, as well as four outspread arms and a line of repeated diamond-shaped motifs. The piece dates from the end of the eighteenth century.

The second fragment is a polychromatic cushion, using three colors—dark carmine red, dark blue, and straw yellow—on an ivory cotton ground. The reverse shows non–counted-thread embroidery in *point de feston* and a crossed chevron stitch. Here the "heads" are larger and squarer with finely serrated edges. There are only two arms, lowered rather than outstretched. A band crowned with multicolored, branching, jagged motifs runs partially around the edges of the piece. Two vaguely round appendages are visible on the skirt. The piece dates from the late-eighteenth or early-nineteenth century.

The third piece is also a fragment of a cushion end. It is decorated with polychromatic work in a range of colors based on three main hues—dark carmine red, dark blue, straw yellow—but also incorporating orange, sky blue, green, brown, two shades of pale red, and violet. As above, the support is ivory cotton canvas, decorated using satin stitch and crossed chevron stitch, enclosed at both ends by a strip of jagged polychromatic motifs that partially extend around the edges of the piece and are topped by a large arborescent motif. The arms are no longer featured. The piece dates from the early-twentieth century.

The three pieces illustrate the clear but progressive evolution in the color palette used and the gradual stylization of the anthropomorphic silhouettes prior to their ultimate disappearance.

Facing page (top): *Maddha* (cushion), Rabat, late-seventeenth century, monochromatic red silk floss with a fine downy finish on cotton, looped stitch, feather stitch, chain stitch, length 34 in. (87 cm), width 13 in. (34 cm), collection of Mr. and Mrs. Niblack, Indianapolis Museum of Art.
Facing page (center): *Maddha* (cushion), Rabat, early-eighteenth century, silk embroidery on cotton, length 20 in. (50 cm), width 22 cm, collection of Mr. and Mrs. Niblack, Indianapolis Museum of Art.
Facing page (bottom): *Maddha* (cushion), Rabat, early-nineteenth century, silk embroidery on cotton, length 27 in. (68 cm), width 16 ½ in. (42 cm), collection of Mr. and Mrs. Niblack, Indianapolis Museum of Art.
Page 148 and 149: *Chest cover,* Rabat, late-eighteenth century, natural polychromatic silk on cotton, back stitch, feather stitch, looped stitch, length 4 ft. 3 in. (130 cm), width 35 in. (90 cm), private collection.

Pages 150 and 151: *Izar* (door hanging), Rabat, early-nineteenth century, polychromatic natural-silk floss with downy finish, on re-embroidered tulle, satin stitch, feather stitch, length 10 ft. (320 cm), width 5 ft. 8 in. (176 cm), private collection.
Pages 152 and 153: *Details of embroidered door hangings*, Rabat, early-nineteenth century, private collection.
Facing page and above: *Chest cover*, Rabat, early-nineteenth century, polychromatic silk floss on re-embroidered cotton muslin, satin stitch, length 5 ft. 2 in. (160 cm), width 35 in. (90 cm), private collection.
Pages 156 and 157: *Izar* (door hanging) featuring an embroidery design known as "the gardens," Rabat, nineteenth century, polychromatic silk embroidery on silk muslin re-embroidered with gold thread, satin and back stitch, pom-pom fringe, length 9 ft. 5 in. (290 cm), width 5 ft. 4 in. (166 cm), private collection.

Facing page and above: *Rzma* (square for making a bundle), Rabat, nineteenth century, monochromatic silk embroidery on cotton,
line stitch, satin stitch, feather stitch, length 4 ft. 7 in. (144 cm), width 4 ft. 7 in. (144 cm), private collection.
Page 160: *Detail of an izar* (door hanging), Rabat, nineteenth century, monochromatic silk embroidery on cotton muslin,
satin stitch, length 13 ft. (400 cm), width 6 ft. 6 in. (200 cm), private collection.
Page 161: *Chest cover*, Rabat, nineteenth century, silk embroidery on cotton, length 3 ft. 7 in. (114 cm), width 3 ft. 3 in. (102 cm), private collection.

Facing page and above: *Chest cover*, Rabat, nineteenth century, silk embroidery on cotton damask, length 4 ft. 3 in. (130 cm), width 3 ft. 1 in. (95 cm), private collection.
Pages 164–165: *Izar* (door hanging), Rabat, nineteenth century, monochromatic silk floss embroidery on polychromatic embroidered linen, length 9 ft. 3 in. (282 cm), width 5 ft. 4 in. (162 cm), private collection.

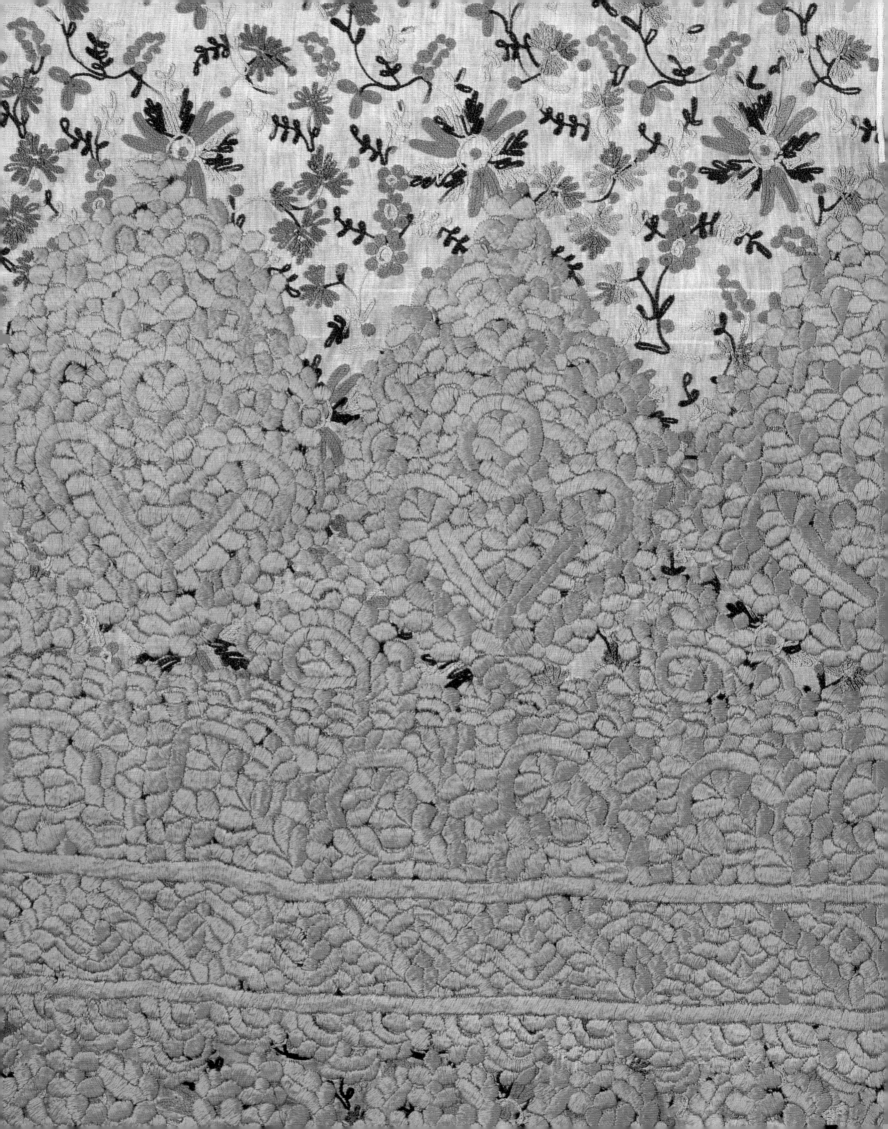

SALÉ

RIOTOUS RESTRAINT

The monochromatic designs featured are imbued with an architectural sense of harmony and balance. Polychromatic cushions feature arborescent geometric motifs, often in bright, cheerful colors. Some pieces feature a profuse mix of geometric motifs, such as squares, diamonds, triangles, and hexagons, set into borders or the edges of designs.

SALÉ

MOROCCAN TEXTILE EMBROIDERY

Situated opposite Rabat on the Bou Regreg estuary, Salé was founded by the Almohads in the twelfth century and cultivated close commercial links with Venice, Geneva, England, and the Low Countries. The city became a notorious base for corsairs in the sixteenth century, and its port was also the haunt of pirates, whose active involvement in the trading of slaves of all origins swelled the local harems. The city's prosperity increased further in the seventeenth century with the arrival of refugees from Muslim Spain. Entire families from Castile, Catalonia, Andalusia, and Murcia settled on the banks of the Bou Regreg, the last of the successive waves of Muslim immigrants driven out of Spain by decree of the Christian king, Philip III. Morocco's new masters, the Alids, were careful to protect the activities of the corsairs. The city's history is clearly reflected in the diverse influences seen in Salé embroideries, which were used to decorate household items such as cushions and door hangings.

Work produced in the twin cities of Rabat and Salé feature comparable red-based color palettes, but distinctive decorative designs. Unlike Rabat work, which uses underdrawing, Salé has produced counted-thread embroideries using the same stitches as those of Chechaouen (running stitch, bouclé, plaited, and cross stitch). Door hangings were embroidered using the

bouclé technique (known as "old Salé"), so that the designs were visible from both sides. On nonreversible cushion covers, motifs are filled with plaited stitch and outlined in isolated cross stitches ("modern Salé").

The city's prolific production of cushion covers falls into two categories, namely monochromatic and polychromatic. Of these, the monochromatic pieces are the most characteristic, featuring designs imbued with an architectural sense of harmony and balance. Polychromatic cushions feature arborescent geometric motifs, often in bright, cheerful colors. Some pieces feature a profuse mix of geometric motifs, such as squares, diamonds, triangles, and hexagons, set into borders or the edges of designs.

Monochromatic cushions, often in brick-red carmine or intense navy blue, are elongated in form and decorated on both sides. The decoration is concentrated around the ends, and the composition remains standard: a band or frieze outlined by a thin strip.

Polychromatic cushions use a wider range of fabrics and colors. Their palette is centered on the four basics—red, blue, yellow, and green—modulated with softer hues. A second type is characterized by a longer, narrower shape, decorated with just two or three colors in a subtle range of hues: navy blue, gray-green or blue-green, eggplant, and carmine red.

Salé's embroidered door hangings have the soft, velvety aspect of certain Chechaouen pieces and are

Page 167: *Khamiya* (curtain, detail), Salé, late-seventeenth century, polychromatic silk embroidery (predominantly red and blue) on linen, looped stitch with cut-outs and drawn-thread *rivière*, length 9 ft. 8 in. (300 cm), width 35 in. (89 cm), private collection.
Facing page: *Young Bride from Rabat*, 1930, photograph by Jean Besancenot (1902–1992), Institut du Monde Arabe, Paris.

worked using the same bouclé technique. The embroidered area covers the bottom of the curtain, spreading across the whole of its width (around 6 ft. 6 in. [200 cm]), to a depth of between 12 and 16 inches (30 and 40 cm). The arborescent friezes feature cypress trees represented by stylized alternating stepped and fringed motifs. The two-color friezes—in navy blue, brick red, or rosewood—also feature arborescent motifs. Martha Guérard provides a fine description: "Sober and refined, the harmonious two-tone color palette is relieved by small polychromatic touches in the central band. In addition to these friezes, the decorative scheme comprises a band, diamonds, highly geometrized floral elements based on cruciform flowers, a drawn-thread *rivière*, three or four colored strips, two fine strips of braid. The door hangings consist mostly of three panels, embroidered separately and subsequently sewn together along their length."

Certain motifs on the door hangings of Salé are reminiscent of the "stork" motifs seen in counted-thread embroideries produced at the same period in Fez. Commenting on the highly stylized motifs of Salé work, Martha Guérard describes "a surprising appendage, the vestige of an earlier motif, apparently the representation of a living creature, reproduced unconsciously here and transformed through copying." She questions if it could be a bird, "the fantastical product of an individual embroiderer's imagination or legacy of a far-distant tradition?"

In perfect condition, the large, complete Salé door hanging illustrated on pages 176–177 is an excellent illustration of the features described above. It is, however, characterized by its fresh colors and extremely fine embroidery. The piece dates from the early-twentieth century.

Facing page: *Long mesned* (cushion), Salé, eighteenth century, monochromatic brick-red silk on ivory linen, looped stitch, length 3 ft. 4 in. (104 cm), width 30 in. (77 cm), private collection.
Pages 172 and 173: *Maddha* (cushion), Salé, early-nineteenth century, polychromatic silk (predominantly carmine red) on thick cotton, plaited stitch, cross stitch, length 4 ft. 3 in. (130 cm), width 29 in. (73 cm), private collection.

SALÉ

Above (top): *Cushion end*, Salé, eighteenth century, monochromatic silk embroidery, plaited stitch, cross stitch, length 33 in. (85 cm), width 18 in. (45 cm), private collection.
Above (bottom): *Cushion end*, Salé, eighteenth century, monochromatic silk embroidery, plaited stitch, cross stitch, line stitch, length 26 in. (66 cm), width 9 in. (22 cm), collection of Mr. and Mrs. Niblack, Indianapolis Museum of Art.

SALÉ

MOROCCAN TEXTILE EMBROIDERY

Above: *Chelliga* (sampler), Salé, eighteenth century, silk embroidery on linen, line stitch, plaited stitch, cross stitch, length 30 in. (75 cm), width 22 in. (55 cm), collection of Mr. and Mrs. Niblack, Indianapolis Museum of Art.
Pages 176–177: *Khamiya* (curtain), Salé, late-seventeenth century, polychromatic silk embroidery (predominantly red and blue) on linen, looped stitch, cut-outs and drawn-thread *rivières*, length 10 ft. (300 cm), width 35 in (89 cm), private collection.

AZEMMOUR

MOROCCAN RENAISSANCE

Azemmour today is an almost perfectly preserved Maghreb town. Slumbering beside the ocean and the *wadi* (estuary), its small, box-shaped white houses and superb gardens, rich with pomegranates, henna, and olive trees, nestle within magnificent ocher-colored ramparts.

ittle can be known about or proved of Azemmour's earliest history, although it may have been a port of call for the seafarers of ancient Carthage. The first settlers at the mouth of the Oum er-Rbia, one of Morocco's largest rivers, were an ancient Berber tribe, the Doukkala. We also know that around 1376, the Marinid Sultan Abd al-Rahman took control of the city but was chased out a year later by his rival, Abu al-Abbas Ahmed, the ruler of Fez. Azemmour maintained close links with Portugal for a time from 1486, when Juan II established an agent in the city to represent his interests.

In Azemmour, the Portuguese bought wheat, horses, *djellabas* (caftan-like garments for Moroccan men), and *haïks* (sari-like wraps worn by Moroccan women), which they either imported back to Portugal or exchanged further down the West African coast for slaves and gold. Relations between Azemmour and Portugal deteriorated from 1502, however, and after a number of diplomatic expeditions and attempts at reconciliation, the Portuguese were forced to leave the city in 1541.

In the past, Azemmour was home to a highly prosperous Jewish population, now long departed, leaving only a number of ruined houses. Azemmour today—still known in Morocco as Moulay Bouchaïb, from the name of its patron saint—is an almost perfectly preserved Maghreb town. Slumbering beside the ocean and the *wadi* (estuary), its small, box-shaped white houses and superb gardens, rich with pomegranates, henna, and olive trees, nestle within magnificent ocher-colored ramparts.

Jeanne Jouin has done much to clarify our understanding of the city's distinctive embroideries, which, in terms of their support, decoration, and technique, are quite unlike anything else in Morocco. Azemmour embroideries are worked on ecru linen bands, between 4 and 20 inches (10 and 40 cm) wide and some 7 feet (200 cm) long. Used as hangings, and as trimmings for curtains and mattresses, they were executed by Jewish women in beautiful crimson red and dark blue silks, using plaited stitch to fill the larger forms, and cross stitch for certain isolated motifs. The ground is completely covered with thick, quilt-like embroidery, so that the design emerges in the parts left "white" (like a negative photograph, as Jeanne Jouin observes). Lively if stylized figurative motifs of animals and birds ("a veritable anomaly in Moroccan arts") are outlined in couched black thread, occupying the central panel of a horizontal, tripartite scheme. Some compositions are based on a central motif of birds with unfurled wings, flanked by calyx-shaped vases supporting three florets. This sometimes alternates with a stylized decorative plant motif or a

Page 179: *Hentlit* (bedcover or wall hanging), Azemmour, late-seventeenth or early-eighteenth century, red and black silk embroidery on linen, line stitch and plaited stitch, length 8 ft. (230 cm), width 4 ft. (120 cm), private collection.
Facing page: *Young Woman with a Mirror*, 1930, photograph by Jean Besancenot (1902–1992), Institut du Monde Arabe, Paris.

female silhouette with a billowing skirt and outstretched arms. Other motifs are birds, chimeras, hieratic dragons, lions (their heads turned back toward their tails), and riders astride curious unicorn-like creatures—all reminiscent of motifs in sixteenth-century Spanish and Italian embroideries. Other compositions feature broad, highly stylized foliated patterns incorporating mythical creatures.

According to Jeanne Jouin: "The little woman with billowing skirts who appears as a secondary motif in certain pieces from Azemmour has traveled the world, from Russia and Spain to Sweden and Norway, and suffered the most extraordinary treatment on her travels. Originally, as a fine lady on Venetian lace, she was accompanied by a falconer and a young lord who offered her a rose. This is a familiar and popular theme in European Renaissance decoration and folk art alike."

The Portuguese occupation of Azemmour bequeathed to the little city not only Andalusian Jewish and Muslim refugees but also northern European slaves. As such, Azemmour embroideries perfectly illustrate the swirling influences that circled the Mediterranean basin.

The present work seeks to provide a flavor of traditional urban life in Morocco, through the study of the embroideries produced by Moroccan women for use and display in their homes. After years of decline, embroidery in Morocco is now experiencing a tentative renaissance, with the creation of a number of workshops in the larger cities, producing items in response to the growing demand from discerning travelers for authentic examples of this superb indigenous artform.

Chelliga (sampler), nineteenth century. Note the Azemmour motifs worked in running stitch and plaited stitch, length 3 ft. 4 in. (103 cm), width 29 in. (73.5 cm), Victoria and Albert Museum.

AZEMMOUR

MOROCCAN TEXTILE EMBROIDERY

Above: *Hentlit* (bedcover or wall hanging), Azemmour, late-seventeenth or early-eighteenth century, length 30 in. (75 cm), width 12 in. (30 cm), private collection.
Facing page: *Arid* (wall hanging), Azemmour, late-seventeenth century, silk embroidery on linen, length 8 ft. 9 in. (271 cm), width 3 ft. 6 in. (109 cm), collection of Mr. and Mrs. Niblack, Indianapolis Museum of Art.
Page 186: *Hentlit* (bedcover or wall hanging), Azemmour, late-seventeenth century, silk embroidery on linen, length 7 ft. 3 in. (224 cm), width 16 in. (41 cm), private collection.
Page 187: *Hentlit* (bedcover or wall hanging, detail), Azemmour, seventeenth century, private collection.
Pages 188-189: *Arid* (wall hanging), Azemmour, seventeenth century, silk embroidery on linen, plaited stitch, line stitch, back stitch, cross stitch, length 7 ft. 3 in. (224 cm), width 4 ft. 2 in. (126 cm), private collection.

Aubin, Eugène. *Le Maroc d'Aujourd'hui*. Paris: Armand Colin, 1912.

Babin, Gustave. *Au Maroc, par les camps et par les villes*. Paris: Grasset, 1912.

Bernes, Jean-Pierre. *Les Broderies Marocaines*. Paris: A, B, C Décor, 1974.

Brignon, Jean. *Histoire du Maroc*. Paris: Hatier, 1967.

Brunot David, Christiane. *Les Broderies de Rabat*. Vols. 1 and 2. Rabat: Institut des Hautes Études Marocaines, 1943.

Burchhardt, Titus. *Moorish Culture in Spain*. London: G. Allen and Unwin Ltd, 1972.

Cumbreno, Floriano. *El bordada – Artes Decoratives Espagnoles*. Barcelona: Alberto Martin, 1942.

Diehl, Charles. *L'Afrique Byzantine, Histoire de la Domination Byzantine en Afrique*. Paris: Leroux, 1896.

Diehl, Charles. *Manuel de l'Art Byzantin*. Paris: n.p., 1925.

Encyclopédie de l'Islam. "Al Andalus" by L. Torres-Balbas. Paris: G. P. Maisonneuve, 1960.

Gayot, H., and Mme Minault. *Les Broderies de Salé*. Rabat: École du Livre, 1955.

Gayot, H., and Mme Minault. *Les Broderies de Meknès*. Rabat: École du Livre, 1956.

Gayot, H., and Mme Minault. *Les Broderies de Fez*. Rabat: École du Livre, 1959.

Goichon, Anne-Marie. "La Broderie au Fil d'Or à Fez." *Hesperis* (1939).

Golvin, L. *Aspects de l'Artisanat en Afrique du Nord*. Paris: PUF, 1958.

Guérard, Martha. "Contribution à l'Étude de l'Art de la Broderie au Maroc," *Hesperis* (1967, 1968, 1969, 1978, 1979).

Hainault, Jean, and Terrasse, Henri. *Les Arts Décoratifs au Maroc*. Paris: H. Laurent, 1925.

Hamet, Ismaïl. *Histoire du Maghreb*. Paris: Leroux, 1928.

Joly, A. *L'Industrie à Tétouan, Broderies de Soie sur Étoffes*. Paris: Leroux, 1908.

Jouin, Jeanne. "Iconographie de la mariée citadine dans l'islam nord-africain." *Revue des Études Islamiques* (1931).

Jouin, Jeanne. "Les Thèmes Décoratifs des Broderies Marocaines. Leur Caractère et leurs Origines." *Hesperis* (1932–35).

Lacomba, Segura. *Bordados Populares Espagnoles*. Madrid: n.p., 1949.

Marçais, Georges. "Les Broderies Turques d'Alger." *Arts Islamica* (1937).

Marçais, Georges. *L'Art musulman*. Paris: n.p., 1962.

Olagnier–Riottot, M. *Influence Turque dans la Broderie de Tétouan au Maroc*. Ankara, Turkey: International Congress on Turkish Art, 1961.

Olagnier–Riottot, M. "Six Brocarts, Ceintures de Femmes, Fez, Tétouan, XVIe–XVIIIe." *Bulletin du Centre d'Études des Textiles Anciens* (1972).

Ricard, Prosper. *Le Souq el Mortgane et les Broderies de Fès*. n.p., 1916.

Ricard, Prosper. *Les Arts Citadins et les Arts Ruraux dans l'Afrique du Nord*. n.p., 1917.

Ricard, Prosper. *Les Arts Marocains de la Broderie*. Algiers: Carbonel, 1918.

Ricard, Prosper. *Pour Comprendre l'Art Musulman dans l'Afrique du Nord et en Espagne*. Paris: Hachette, 1924.

Ricard, Prosper. *Dentelles Algériennes et Marocaines*. Paris: Librairie Larose, 1928.

Ricard, Prosper. "Broderies de Soie." *Nord-Sud* (1934).

Rousseau, G. *L'Art Décoratif Musulman*. Paris: Marcel Rivière, 1934.

Soustiel, Joseph. *L'Art Turc, Céramiques, Tapis, Étoffes, Velours, Broderies*. Paris: La Colombe, 1952.

Spring, Christopher, and Hudson, Julie. *North African Textiles*. London: British Museum, 1995.

Stone, Caroline. *The Embroideries of North Africa*. London: Longman, 1985.

Terrasse, Henri. *L'Art Hispano-Mauresque des Origines au XIIIe siècle*. Paris: Van Oest, 1932.

Terrasse, Henri. *Histoire du Maroc*. Casablanca: n.p., 1950.

Vicaire, M. "Les Brocarts de Fez." *Nord-Sud* (n.d.).

Vivier, Marie-France. *Broderies Marocaines*. Paris: RMN, 1991.

Vivier, Marie-France. "Les Broderies," in *De Soie et d'Or*. Paris: Institut du Monde Arabe, 1996.

Vivier, Marie-France. "La Broderie," in *Maroc, les Trésors du Royaume*. Paris: Petit Palais, 1999.

Wace, A. J. B. *Mediterranean and Near Eastern Embroideries*. London: Halton and Co., 1935.

Catalogs

Catalogue of Algerian Embroideries. London: Victoria and Albert Museum, Department of Textiles, 1915.

De Soie and d'Or: Broderies du Maghreb. Paris: Institut du Monde Arabe, 1996.

Florilèges de Soie: les Broderies d'Alger. Paris: Institut du Monde Arabe, 1993.

Les Arts du Maghreb, fin XVIIIe, début XIXe. Brussels: n.p., 1973.

Maroc, les Trésors du Royaume. Paris: Petit Palais, 1999.

Noces Tissées, Noces Brodées. Parures et Costumes Féminins de Tunisie. Paris: MAAO, 1995.

Turkish Folk Embroideries. London: Museum of Mankind, 1981.

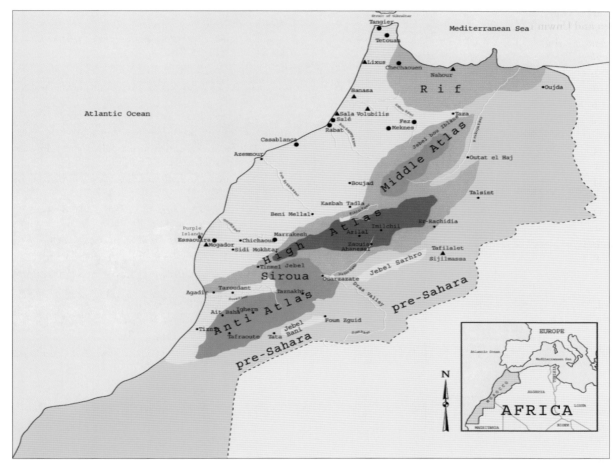

Map courtesy of the Indianapolis Museum of Art.

Photographic Credits

black and white photographs: p. 8: Photo Gabriel Veyre © Collection Jacquier-Veyre; pp.17, 18, 23, 27, 30, 47, 74, 98: © Private collection/All rights reserved; pp. 35, 39, 94, 104, 128, 140, 168, 180: Photo Jean Besancenot © Photothèque IMA/Besancenot; p. 145 © Roger Viollet.

color photographs: p. 52: © Indianapolis Museum of Art.

paintings: p.12: © Private collection/All rights reserved; pp. 21, 44, 48: © ACR/All rights reserved.

textiles: p. 57 © TBE Iletism ve Yayincilik A.S., Istanbul; pp. 85, 183: © Victoria and Albert Museum; p. 88: © Musée des Tissus, Lyon/Sylvain Pretto; pp. 102 (bottom), 135, 147, 174 (bottom), 175, 185: © Indianapolis Museum of Art/The Eliza M. and Sarah L. Niblack Collection.

I would particularly like to thank

Marie-France Vivier, director of the Maghreb section of the Musée des Arts d'Afrique and d'Océanie
in Paris, and of museography of the North African section of the Musée du quai Branly,
who gave me invaluable access to her department's collections and resources, and generous
advice based on her own extensive expertise.

I would also like to thank Sandrine Balihaut Martin, my editor at Flammarion,
for her enthusiasm and efficiency.

Thank you to Emmanuel Laparra and Pierre Ferbos for their excellent work,
the Indianapolis Museum of Art, l'Institut du Monde Arabe, the Victoria and Albert Museum,
the Musée des Textiles de Lyon, les Editions ACR, the Roger Viollet agency, Jacques Veyre,
and all the collectors who wished to remain anonymous.

I am enormously indebted to Christiane Brunot-David, Jeanne Jouin, and Martha Guérard for their
passionate work in this field. I wish to give special thanks to them.

I am grateful to my family, for their unfailing support throughout all my research.

I would also like to thank the many people who provided much-needed
encouragement and enabled me to write this book:
Wendy and Francis Abeberry, Geneviève Aiche, Mina Aït Ali,
Harb Al Zuhair, Tallal and Sarah Al Zuhair, Françoise Ayxandri,
Suzy Amman, Abdelilah Azmi, Hélène Bercovitz, Mel Byars, Jean François Coulomb,
Philippe Delattre, Sandy and Babou Dibon, Mr. and Mme El Fenni,
Thomas Erhman, Berndt Egenberger, Manu Etcheverry,
Olivier Gagnère, Nezha Goundiz, Caroline Haardt de La Baume,
Betsy and Morris Hyams, Nicolas Junod, Jean Claude Laborde, Suline Lapat,
Agnès Léglise, Jean Louis Lembascher, Anne Marchalle, Cathy Orfanos, Bernard Ossude,
Lady Petunia, Joclyn Souty, Lillebi Taittinger, Catherine Trémot,
Philipe Verger, Franck Vieljeux, and Sidi Chaouen.